Appalachian Trail
Data Book
1997

D1085913

Appalachian Trail Data Book 1997

Nineteenth Edition

Daniel D. Chazin

The Appalachian Trail Conference
Harpers Ferry

Contents

Notice to All Trail Users

The information in this publication is the result of the best effort of the publisher, using data available to it at the time of printing. Changes resulting from maintenance work and relocations are constantly occurring and, therefore, no published route can be regarded as precisely accurate at the time you read this notice.

Notices of pending relocations are indicated in current Appalachian Trail guidebooks. Because maintenance of the Trail is conducted by volunteers and maintaining clubs listed in the appropriate guidebooks, questions about the exact route of the Trail should be addressed to the maintaining clubs or the Appalachian Trail Conference, P.O. Box 807, Harpers Ferry, W.Va. 25425 (telephone: 304-535-6331). On the Trail, please pay close attention to—and follow—the white blazes and any directional signs.

Responsibility for Safety

It is extremely important to plan your hike, especially in places where water is scarce. Purify water drawn from any source. Water purity cannot be guaranteed. The Appalachian Trail Conference and the various maintaining clubs attempt to locate good sources of water along the Trail but have no control over these sources and cannot, in any sense, be responsible for the quality of the water at any given time. You should ensure the safety of all water you use by treating it.

Certain risks are inherent in any Appalachian Trail hike. Each A.T. user must accept personal responsibility for his or her safety while on the Trail. The Appalachian Trail Conference and its member maintaining clubs cannot ensure the safety of any hiker on the Trail, and, when undertaking a hike on the Trail, each user thereby assumes the risk for any accident, illness, or injury that might occur on the Trail.

Enjoy your hike, but please take all appropriate precautions for your safety and well-being.

Hiker Awareness

Although it is safer on the Appalachian Trail than most places, you should be aware that problems do occur and a few crimes of violence have occurred during the past two decades. **Hiker Awareness** is one of your best lines of defense. Be aware of what you are doing, where you are, and to whom you are talking. Here are some suggestions:

• **Don't hike alone.** If you are by yourself and encounter a stranger who makes you feel uncomfortable, say you are with a group that is behind you. Be creative. If in doubt, move on.

• **Leave** your hiking **itinerary** and **timetable** with **someone** at home. Be sure he or she knows your Trail name, if you have one. Check in regularly, and establish a procedure to follow if you fail to check in. It helps to let ATC know your name and Trail name, in case a family member needs to reach you.

• **Be wary of strangers.** Be friendly, but cautious. Don't tell strangers your plans. Avoid people who act suspiciously, hostile, or intoxicated.

• **Don't camp near road crossings.**

• **Dress conservatively** to avoid unwanted attention.

• Carrying **firearms** is **strongly discouraged.** They are illegal on National Park Service lands and in most other areas without a permit, they could be turned against you, you face a high risk of an accidental shooting, and they are extra weight.

• **Eliminate opportunities for theft.** Don't bring jewelry. Hide your money. If you must leave your pack, hide it carefully, or leave it with someone trustworthy. Don't leave valuables or equipment (especially in sight) in vehicles parked at Trailheads.

• **Use the Trail and shelter registers.** Sign in, leave a note, and report any suspicious activities. If someone needs to locate you, or if a serious crime has been committed along the Trail, the first place authorities will look is in the registers.

• **Report** any **crime** or **harassment** to the local law-enforcement authorities and ATC. Use the incident report form on page 69; cut out, fold, and mail it to ATC.

As the Trail becomes better known and grows in popularity, it is likely that vagrants, vandals, and ruffians will be around. Let's do our best to keep the Trail a safe place. Maintain your **Hiker Awareness**, help each other, and report all incidents. In this way, together we can be a more effective "community deterrent." Be prudent and cautious without allowing common sense to slip into paranoia.

Preface

This publication provides a ready reference for hikers to the major features of the Appalachian Trail as it winds for more than 2,150 miles from Maine to Georgia. Many hikers find it indispensable to their journey(s) throughout the year on the A.T. and save each year's edition as a record of their experiences and accomplishments.

The features listed here include shelters and campsites, road crossings, sources of water, principal mountain peaks and gaps, and other notable physical landmarks of America's first national scenic trail. Locations of areas where lodging, meals, groceries, and post offices are available also are listed, with distances and directions to them indicated.

The *Data Book* is intended to be useful in broad-scale planning of a trip of any length on the Trail, from home or while on the footpath itself.

The *Data Book* does not, however, include sufficient detail for careful, complete planning of a trip. Potential hikers are encouraged to purchase separately the *Appalachian Trail Guide* for the state(s) they plan to hike. The guidebooks contain detailed descriptions of Trail sections, facilities near the Trail, points of interest off the Trail, background on the history and natural features of the area, and other important information.

All guidebooks are sold with sets of maps for the state(s) described, another key to an enjoyable hike. Guidebooks, maps, and other ATC publications may be ordered by telephone—(304) 535-6331—or by writing the Appalachian Trail Conference, P.O. Box 807, Harpers Ferry, W.Va. 25425. A catalogue of publications and merchandise is available upon request. Membership in the Appalachian Trail Conference carries with it a discount on guidebooks and other publications.

The compilation of each edition of the *Data Book* begins with the latest *Appalachian Trail Guides*. The distances and descriptive information are updated to take into account relocations since the last edition.

This information is supplied to the Conference by its member clubs and individuals who maintain the Trail on a volunteer basis all year to help ensure access to the Appalachian Trail experience for all.

The data has been cross-checked by both volunteers and staff members. However, it is impossible to ensure absolute accuracy of the information, and changes may occur during the year of this edition. Trail-enhancing relocations that affect distances between major features are underway in many states. Also, severe weather conditions, fires, and other unpredictable developments might affect the condition of the Trail and force temporary closings of a section.

Users of the Trail for any period of time should carefully follow the painted white blazes that mark the current route of the Trail.

Hikers finding errors or omissions in the *Data Book* are urged to report them to ATC's publications department, at the address above, so the appropriate changes can be included in the next edition.

The continued existence of the Appalachian Trail depends, in part, on proper use by those who walk on it. Particular care should be taken not to damage the footpath itself, natural features (geological or botanical) alongside it, or the property of others, through littering or other vandalism, improper fires, or use of vehicles. The needs of other users should always be considered, and special regulations must be followed in many areas. Please keep dayhiking groups to 25 persons or less and overnight groups to no more than 10 persons.

Although more than 98 percent of the Appalachian Trail now crosses public land, the remainder is on private property, thanks to the cooperation and good faith of the landowners. The Conference and its member clubs strongly urge all users of the Trail to respect these private lands and the owners' rights as if they were their own.

Public lands are, in a sense, the user's own—shared with all other users—so please proceed accordingly, taking care to obey any regulations imposed on use of the Trail in a particular section.

For example, camping permits are required before entering Great Smoky Mountains National Park. In New Hampshire, camping is permitted around shelters only when specifically stated. On many other parts of the Trail, camping is permitted only in designated areas.

Again, please consult the guidebooks, and watch for special signs along the Trail.

Reporting Trail Emergencies

Check the guidebook, nearest shelter, or Trailhead facility for local emergency telephone numbers and the location of the nearest telephone. Leave the Trail at the nearest road crossing, and find a telephone. Know your location and the location of the incident as precisely as possible. Dial "911" or "0" (ask the operator to connect you with the nearest state-police facility), and make your report. Ask the officer to notify the Appalachian Trail Conference at (304) 535-6331. Also, please fill out the form on page 69, and mail it to ATC from the next post office.

How to Use the *Data Book*

The *Data Book* is divided into eleven chapters, beginning with Maine (at Katahdin) and ending with Georgia (at Springer Mountain). With one exception, each chapter corresponds to a volume in the current series of *Appalachian Trail Guides* (see page x for ordering information). Chapter Three, for example, matches the third volume in the guidebook series, which covers the Trail in Massachusetts-Connecticut. The exception is the Trail route through the Great Smokies of Tennessee and North Carolina, which is covered in both the Tennessee-North Carolina and North Carolina-Georgia guidebooks. It is included here only in Chapter Ten (Tennessee-North Carolina).

Each chapter of the *Data Book* is divided into sections that correspond to the Trail sections as numbered and identified in the corresponding guide (except for Maine). Except for the Shenandoah National Park chapter, sections are numbered consecutively, from north to south, within each state. (Because the *Appalachian Trail Guide to Maine* includes point-to-point Trail descriptions on its maps, but not in the book itself, Chapter One of the *Data Book* identifies sections according to the Maine map on which they appear. The sections in the Shenandoah National Park chapter are numbered independently of the remainder of Virginia, according to the latest edition of the guidebook for the park.) These section numbers are given in the columns to the far left and far right on each page, under the heading "GBS" (guidebook section). For more detail about a particular feature, just look up this section in the appropriate guidebook.

Each section contains a list of features along or near the Trail. Towns are printed in boldface. Towns with post offices carry their ZIP Code in the listing—for example: Vt. 103, **North Clarendon, Vt., P.O. 05759.**

In general, all facilities within five miles of the Trail by road are included, unless similar facilities are located closer to the footpath or a facility's inclusion would not significantly benefit the hiker. In some cases, where a particular facility is not available for a great distance, we have included facilities that are more than five miles from the Trail but still within 10 miles.

To the right of the list of features, facilities, if any, are noted with a one-letter code. These codes are explained on pages xv-xvi.

Except for shelters, campsites, and water sources located on the Trail itself—or within 0.1 mile of the footpath—the listing for a facility includes the distance and direction to it. So, if the symbols "C", "S", or "w" appear without direction and distance information in the listing, that campsite, shelter, or water source is on the Trail or within about 500 feet of it.

The number to the left of a feature is the distance—in miles—of the feature from the northern end of the part of the Trail covered in that particular chapter (read down). The number to the right of the features and facilities lists, correspondingly, is the feature's distance from the southern end of the part of the Trail covered by this chapter (read up). The starting point for the cumulative distance is given at the top of the column.

Sometimes the Trail follows a road, ridge line, lake, creek, or other physical feature for some distance. In these cases, usually only one distance is listed. For roads, this is generally the point at which the Trail first reaches the road proceeding from north to south, or, in some cases, the point representing the end of the section. For ridge lines, this is the highest point. Again, for more complete information about a particular feature, please consult the guidebooks and/or maps.

Abbreviations

These abbreviations are used in the "Facilities" columns of the listings that follow:

C   Campsites and campgrounds. Unless otherwise indicated, water is available. For New Hampshire, the "C" code is also used to indicate those shelters at which camping is permitted.

E   "East," used to designate direction to facilities that are to the right of the Trail when traveling north.

G   Groceries, supplies.

GBS   Guidebook section.

L   Lodgings other than Trail shelters, campsites, and campgrounds: for example, motels, hotels, cottages, and hostels. This code is also used for the Appalachian Mountain Club (AMC) huts in New Hampshire and camps (commercial cottages) in Maine.

m   Miles.

M   Meals; restaurants.

nw   No potable water. This is used in shelter and campsite listings only.

P.O.   Post office. Towns without post offices are listed only if the Trail goes directly through them; "P.O." is omitted in these cases.

R   Road access. Only roads open to the public and passable by ordinary automobiles are designated. Included are road crossings and locations where the Trail runs along a road or is adjacent to a road that provides access to the Trail. Where the road crossings are frequent (every two miles or less), lesser ones are omitted.

S   Shelter. A three-sided structure, with or without bunks or floors, intended as overnight housing for hikers. Also known as lean-tos in many areas. Included in this category are unlocked cabins or lodges, found primarily in New Hampshire, Vermont, Pennsylvania, and Maryland.

W   "West," used to designate direction to facilities that are to the left of the Trail when traveling north.

w   Water (from springs, streams, *etc.*). In general, where available, water sources are listed about every three to four miles. Other water sources do exist, and not every water source is listed in the *Data Book.* **Note: All water should be purified before use.**

The Appalachian Trail
– End to End –
Length by Section

These sections and Trail points correspond to the beginnings and endings of chapters in this book and the eleven-volume series of *Appalachian Trail Guides*.

Maine 281.4
New Hampshire-Vermont 306.6
Massachusetts-Connecticut 141.8
New York-New Jersey 161.8
Pennsylvania 232.0
Maryland-Northern Virginia 94.2
Shenandoah National Park 106.9
Central Virginia 220.6
Southwest Virginia 162.6
Tennessee-North Carolina 288.8
North Carolina-Georgia 163.5

Cumulative Distances

	Miles North to South	Miles South to North
Baxter Peak, Katahdin, Maine	0.0	2,160.2
Maine-New Hampshire Line	281.4	1,878.8
Vermont-Massachusetts Line	588.0	1,572.2
Connecticut-New York Line	729.8	1,430.4
New Jersey-Pennsylvania Line	891.6	1,268.6
Pennsylvania-Maryland Line	1,123.6	1,036.6
Front Royal, Virginia	1,217.8	942.4
Rockfish Gap, Virginia	1,324.7	835.5
New River, Virginia	1,545.3	614.9
Damascus, Virginia	1,707.9	452.3
Fontana Dam, North Carolina	1,996.7	163.5
Springer Mountain, Georgia	2,160.2	0.0

Maine

G B S	North to South	FEATURES	Facilities (See page xv for codes)	South to North	G B S
	Miles from Katahdin			*Miles from Maine-N.H. Line*	
♦	0.0	Katahdin (Baxter Peak)		281.4	♦
	1.0	Thoreau Spring	w	280.4	
	4.0	Katahdin Stream Falls	w	277.4	
	5.2	Katahdin Stream Campground (C,L,S,w on A.T.)	CLSw	276.2	
	5.3	Perimeter Road	R	276.1	
	7.6	Daicey Pond Campground (C,L,S,w on A.T.)	RCLSw	273.8	
	8.8	Big Niagara Falls	w	272.6	
	10.3	Baxter State Park Boundary		271.1	
	11.0	Pine Point	w	270.4	
	13.2	Foss and Knowlton Brook	w	268.2	
	14.0	Katahdin Stream	w	267.4	
♦	15.1	Abol Bridge over West Branch of Penobscot River (C,G,w on A.T.)	RCGw	266.3	♦
	18.6	Hurd Brook Lean-to	Sw	262.8	
	21.1	Rainbow Ledges		260.3	
	22.9	Rainbow Lake (east end)	w	258.5	
	26.3	Rainbow Spring Campsite	Cw	255.1	
	28.1	Rainbow Lake (west end)	w	253.3	
	30.1	Rainbow Stream Lean-to	Sw	251.3	
	32.5	Pollywog Stream	w	248.9	
	33.9	Crescent Pond (west end)	w	247.5	
	36.3	Nesuntabunt Mountain		245.1	
	38.2	Wadleigh Stream Lean-to	Sw	243.2	
♦	40.8	Nahmakanta Lake (south end)	Rw	240.6	♦
	44.0	Nahmakanta Stream Campsite	Cw	237.4	
	47.7	Pemadumcook Lake (southwest shore)	w	233.7	
	48.3	Potaywadjo Spring Lean-to	Sw	233.1	
	50.1	Sand Beach, Lower Jo-Mary Lake	w	231.3	
	51.8	Antlers Campsite	Cw	229.6	

Left margin labels: Map 1, Sec. 1 · Map 1, Sec. 2 · Map 2, Sec. 3

Right margin labels: Map 1, Sec. 1 · Map 1, Sec. 2 · Map 2, Sec. 3

MAINE

G B S	North to South	FEATURES	Facilities (See page xv for codes)	South to North	G B S
	Miles from Katahdin			*Miles from Maine-N.H. Line*	
	53.1	Mud Pond (outlet)	w	228.3	
	56.0	Jo-Mary Road (w on A.T.; C,G 6m E)	RCGw	225.4	
	59.7	Cooper Brook Falls Lean-to	Sw	221.7	
	62.0	Crawford Pond (outlet)	w	219.4	
	62.9	Kokadjo-B Pond Road		218.5	
	64.3	Little Boardman Mountain		217.1	
	65.6	Spring	w	215.8	
	65.9	Mountain View Pond (outlet)	w	215.5	
	67.5	East Branch of Pleasant River (ford)	w	213.9	
Map 2, Sec. 3	67.8	East Branch Lean-to	Sw	213.6	Map 2, Sec. 3
	69.8	West Branch Ponds Road (L,M 4m W)	RLM	211.6	
	71.4	Logan Brook Lean-to	Sw	210.0	
	72.8	White Cap Mountain		208.6	
	73.9	White Brook Trail		207.5	
	74.5	Hay Mountain		206.9	
	76.1	West Peak		205.3	
	76.8	Sidney Tappan Campsite	Cw	204.6	
	77.7	Gulf Hagas Mountain		203.7	
	78.6	Carl A. Newhall Lean-to	Sw	202.8	
	82.1	Gulf Hagas Cut-off Trail	w	199.3	
	82.8	Gulf Hagas Trail	w	198.6	
	83.8	The Hermitage (C,w 0.7m E)	Cw	197.6	
◆	84.1	West Branch of Pleasant River (ford)	w	197.3	◆
	84.6	Logging Road	R	196.8	
Map 3, Sec. 4	85.8	East Chairback Pond Side Trail (w 0.2m W)	w	195.6	Map 3, Sec. 4
	88.0	Chairback Mountain		193.4	
	88.5	Chairback Gap Lean-to	Sw	192.9	
	88.9	Columbus Mountain		192.5	
	90.2	West Chairback Pond Side Trail	w	191.2	

G B S	North to South	FEATURES	Facilities (See page xv for codes)	South to North	G B S
	Miles from Katahdin			*Miles from Maine-N.H. Line*	
	90.8	Third Mountain, Monument Cliff		190.6	
	93.3	Fourth Mountain		188.1	
	95.4	Cloud Pond Lean-to Side Trail (S,w 0.3m E)	Sw	186.0	
	96.3	Barren Mountain		185.1	
	99.4	Long Pond Stream Lean-to	Sw	182.0	
Map 3, Sec. 4	100.2	Long Pond Stream (ford)	Sw	181.2	Map 3, Sec. 4
	104.1	Wilson Valley Lean-to	Sw	177.3	
	104.5	Canadian Pacific Railroad		176.9	
	104.8	Big Wilson Stream (ford)	w	176.6	
	107.7	Little Wilson Stream	w	173.7	
	107.9	Little Wilson Falls		173.5	
	110.7	North Pond (outlet)	w	170.7	
	111.5	Leeman Brook Lean-to	Sw	169.9	
	112.6	Lily Pond	w	168.8	
	113.3	Bell Pond	w	168.1	
	114.4	Spectacle Pond (outlet)	w	167.0	
	114.5	Maine 15	R	166.9	
◆	117.8	**Monson, Maine, P.O. 04464** (P.O.,C,G,L,M 2m E)	CGLM	163.6	◆
	120.8	Shirley-Blanchard Road	R	160.6	
	121.2	East Branch of Piscataquis River (ford)	w	160.2	
	123.5	Horseshoe Canyon Lean-to	Sw	157.9	
Map 4, Sec. 5	126.6	West Branch of Piscataquis River (ford)	w	154.8	Map 4, Sec. 5
	130.3	Bald Mountain Pond (outlet)	w	151.1	
	132.4	Moxie Bald Lean-to	Sw	149.0	
	134.5	Moxie Bald Mountain		146.9	
	136.5	Bald Mountain Brook Lean-to	Sw	144.9	
	139.3	Moxie Pond (south end)	Rw	142.1	
	144.2	Pleasant Pond Mountain		137.2	
	145.5	Pleasant Pond Lean-to	Sw	135.9	
	145.9	Boise-Cascade Logging Road	R	135.5	
	148.5	Holly Brook	w	132.9	

MAINE

	Miles from Katahdin			*Miles from Maine-N.H. Line*	
	151.2	U.S. 201; **Caratunk, Maine, P.O. 04925** (P.O.,G 0.3m E; L 1.2m W; C,L,M 2.5m W)	RCGLM	130.2	
◆	151.5	Kennebec River	w	129.9	◆
	154.8	Trail to Harrison's Pierce Pond Camps (L,M 0.3m E; w 0.1m E)	RLMw	126.6	
	155.2	Pierce Pond Lean-to	Sw	126.2	
	158.7	North Branch of Carrying Place Stream	w	122.7	
	159.4	Logging Road	R	122.0	
	161.1	East Carry Pond (north end)	w	120.3	
	162.6	Sandy Stream, Middle Carry Pond (inlet)	w	118.8	
	164.5	West Carry Pond (east side)	w	116.9	
	165.2	West Carry Pond Lean-to	Sw	116.2	
	165.9	West Carry Pond (west side)	w	115.5	
	167.0	Roundtop Mountain		114.4	
◆	168.7	Long Falls Dam Road, Jerome Brook	Rw	112.7	◆
	171.0	Bog Brook Road, Flagstaff Lake (outlet)	Rw	110.4	
	171.1	East Flagstaff Road	R	110.3	
	172.5	Little Bigelow Lean-to	Sw	108.9	
	174.2	Little Bigelow Mountain (east end)		107.2	
	177.4	Safford Notch Campsite (C,w 0.3m E)	Cw	104.0	
	177.5	Safford Brook Trail		103.9	
	179.4	Bigelow Mountain (Avery Peak)		102.0	
	179.8	Myron H. Avery Lean-to, Bigelow Col, Fire Warden's Trail	Sw	101.6	
	180.1	Bigelow Mountain (West Peak)		101.3	
	182.2	South Horn		99.2	
	182.7	Horns Pond Lean-tos	CSw	98.7	
	182.9	Horns Pond Trail		98.5	
	184.6	Bigelow Range Trail, Cranberry Pond (w 0.2m W)	w	96.8	

Map 5, Sec. 6 (left and right margins)
Map 5, Sec. 7 (left and right margins)

G B S	North to South	FEATURES	Facilities (See page xv for codes)	South to North	G B S
	Miles from Katahdin			*Miles from Maine-N.H. Line*	
	185.9	Cranberry Stream Campsite	Cw	95.5	
	186.8	Stratton Brook	w	94.6	
	187.0	Stratton Brook Pond Road	R	94.4	
♦	187.8	Maine 27; **Stratton, Maine, P.O. 04982** (P.O.,G,L,M 5m W)	RGLM	93.6	♦
	193.0	North Crocker Mountain		88.4	
	194.0	South Crocker Mountain		87.4	
	195.1	Crocker Cirque Campsite Side Trail (w on A.T.; C 0.2m E)	Cw	86.3	
	196.1	Caribou Valley Road	R	85.3	
	196.2	South Branch Carrabassett River (ford)	w	85.2	
	198.4	Sugarloaf Mountain Trail		83.0	
	200.5	Spaulding Mountain		80.9	
	201.3	Spaulding Mountain Lean-to	Sw	80.1	
	202.4	Mt. Abraham Trail		79.0	
	203.5	Lone Mountain		77.9	
	206.6	Orbeton Stream (ford)	w	74.8	
	209.3	Poplar Ridge Lean-to	Sw	72.1	
	210.3	Stream	w	71.1	
	210.7	Saddleback Junior		70.7	
	212.7	The Horn		68.7	
	214.3	Saddleback Mountain		67.1	
	216.3	Eddy Pond	w	65.1	
	218.2	Piazza Rock Lean-to	Sw	63.2	
	219.9	Sandy River	w	61.5	
♦	220.0	Maine 4; **Rangeley, Maine, P.O. 04970** (P.O.,C,G,L,M 9m W)	RCGLM	61.4	♦
	222.1	South Pond	w	59.3	
	224.8	Little Swift River Pond Campsite	Cw	56.6	
	229.4	Sabbath Day Pond Lean-to	Sw	52.0	
	231.5	Moxie Pond	w	49.9	
♦	233.1	Maine 17	R	48.3	♦

Map 6, Sec. 8 (left and right margins, rows 198.4–214.3)

Map 6, Sec. 9 (left and right margins, rows 222.1–229.4)

MAINE

G B S	North to South	FEATURES	Facilities (See page xv for codes)	South to North	G B S
	Miles from Katahdin		*Miles from Maine-N.H. Line*		
Map 7, Sec. 10	233.9	Bemis Stream (ford)	w	47.5	Map 7, Sec. 10
	237.7	Bemis Mountain Lean-to	Sw	43.7	
	239.4	Bemis Range (West Peak)		42.0	
	240.4	Bemis Stream Trail		41.0	
	243.6	Old Blue Mountain		37.8	
◆	246.4	South Arm Road, Black Brook (ford) (w on A.T.; C,G 4.5m W)	RCGw	35.0	◆
Map 7, Sec. 11	248.2	Moody Mountain		33.2	Map 7, Sec. 11
	249.1	Sawyer Notch, Sawyer Brook (ford)	w	32.3	
	250.5	Hall Mountain Lean-to	Sw	30.9	
	251.8	Wyman Mountain		29.6	
	254.7	Surplus Pond (outlet)	w	26.7	
◆	256.5	East B Hill Road; **Andover, Maine, P.O. 04216** (P.O.,C,G,L,M 8m E)	RCGLM	24.9	◆
Map 7, Sec. 12	257.3	Dunn Notch and Falls	w	24.1	Map 7, Sec. 12
	261.0	Frye Notch Lean-to	Sw	20.4	
	262.8	Baldpate Mountain (East Peak)		18.6	
	263.7	Baldpate Mountain (West Peak)		17.7	
	264.5	Baldpate Lean-to	Sw	16.9	
◆	266.8	Grafton Notch, Maine 26	R	14.6	◆
	267.9	Brook	w	13.5	
	270.3	Old Speck Trail		11.1	
Map 7, Sec. 13	271.4	Speck Pond Shelter and Campsite, Speck Pond Trail	CSw	10.0	Map 7, Sec. 13
	272.3	Mahoosuc Arm		9.1	
	273.9	Mahoosuc Notch (east end)	w	7.5	
	275.0	Mahoosuc Notch (west end), Mahoosuc Notch Trail	w	6.4	
	276.0	Fulling Mill Mountain (South Peak)		5.4	
	276.5	Full Goose Shelter and Campsite	CSw	4.9	
	277.5	Goose Eye Mountain (North Peak)		3.9	
	278.7	Goose Eye Mountain (East Peak)		2.7	

G B S	North to South	FEATURES	Facilities (See page xv for codes)	South to North	G B S
	Miles from Katahdin			*Miles from Maine-N.H. Line*	
Map 7, Sec. 13	280.5	Mt. Carlo		0.9	Map 7, Sec. 13
	280.9	Carlo Col Trail, Carlo Col Shelter and Campsite (C,S,w 0.3m W)	CSw	0.5	
	281.4	Maine-New Hampshire Line		0.0	

New Hampshire-Vermont

G B S	North to South	FEATURES	Facilities (See page xv for codes)	South to North	G B S
	Miles from Maine-N.H. Line			*Miles from Vt.-Mass. Line*	
◆	0.0	Maine-New Hampshire Line		306.6	◆
	1.9	Mt. Success		304.7	
	4.7	Gentian Pond Campsite	CSw	301.9	
	5.4	Moss Pond	w	301.2	
N.H. 1	6.9	Dream Lake	w	299.7	N.H. 1
	9.6	Trident Col Tentsite	Cw	297.0	
	10.7	Cascade Mountain		295.9	
	15.0	Brook	w	291.6	
	16.2	Androscoggin River	R	290.4	
◆	16.5	U.S. 2; **Gorham, N.H., P.O. 03581** (w on A.T.; P.O.,G,L,M 3.6m W; C,G 1m E; C,L,M 2m W)	RCGLMw	290.1	◆
	18.4	Rattle River Shelter	Sw	288.2	
	22.4	Mt. Moriah		284.2	
	24.5	Imp Campsite	CSw	282.1	
N.H. 2	27.0	Middle Carter Mountain		279.6	N.H. 2
	29.1	Zeta Pass		277.5	
	30.5	Carter Dome		276.1	
	31.0	Spring	w	275.6	
	31.7	Carter Notch, Carter Notch Hut (L,w 0.1m E)	Lw	274.9	
	32.6	Wildcat Mountain, Peak A		274.0	
	34.6	Wildcat Mountain, Peak D		272.0	
◆	37.6	Pinkham Notch, N.H. 16, Pinkham Notch Camp (L,M,w on A.T.)	RLMw	269.0	◆
	39.5	Lowe's Bald Spot		267.1	
N.H. 3	41.6	West Branch, Peabody River	w	265.0	N.H. 3
	42.4	Osgood Tentsite	Cw	264.2	
	44.9	Mt. Madison		261.7	
	45.4	Madison Springs Hut, Valley Way Tentsite (C,w 0.6m W; L,M,w on A.T.)	CLMw	261.2	

G B S	North to South	FEATURES	Facilities (See page xv for codes)	South to North	G B S
	Miles from Maine-N.H. Line			*Miles from Vt.-Mass. Line*	
	46.3	Thunderstorm Junction, Spur Trail to Crag Camp Cabin, Lowe's Path to Mt. Adams & Gray Knob Cabin (C,S,w 1.1m W, 1.2m W)	CSw	260.3	
	46.9	Israel Ridge Path to The Perch Shelter (C,S,w 0.9m W)	CSw	259.7	
	47.6	Edmands Col		259.0	
	51.0	**Mt. Washington, N.H., P.O. 03589** (P.O.,M on A.T.)	RM	255.6	
N.H. 3	52.4	Lakes of the Clouds Hut (L,M,w on A.T.)	LMw	254.2	N.H. 3
	53.9	Mt. Franklin		252.7	
	54.2	Spring	w	252.4	
	55.5	Spring	w	251.1	
	56.4	Mt. Pierce (Mt. Clinton)		250.2	
	57.2	Mizpah Spring Hut, Nauman Tentsite (C,L,M,w on A.T.)	CLMw	249.4	
	58.9	Mt. Jackson		247.7	
	60.3	Mt. Webster		246.3	
	63.5	Saco River		243.1	
♦	63.6	Crawford Notch, U.S. 302, Dry River Campground (C 1.5m E; L 3.7m W; M 1m W)	RCLM	243.0	♦
	66.5	Ethan Pond Campsite	CSw	240.1	
	71.3	Zealand Falls Hut (L,M,w on A.T.)	LMw	235.3	
N.H. 4	72.5	Zeacliff		234.1	N.H. 4
	75.5	Mt. Guyot, Guyot Campsite (C,S,w 0.7m E)	CSw	231.1	
	77.5	South Twin Mountain, North Twin Spur		229.1	
	78.3	Galehead Hut (L,M,w on A.T.)	LMw	228.3	

NEW HAMPSHIRE-VERMONT

G B S	North to South	FEATURES	Facilities (See page xv for codes)	South to North	G B S
	Miles from Maine-N.H. Line		*Miles from Vt.-Mass. Line*		
	81.0	Garfield Ridge Campsite	CSw	225.6	
	81.4	Mt. Garfield		225.2	
N.H. 4	84.9	Mt. Lafayette, Greenleaf Hut (L,M 1.1m W; w 0.2m W)	LMw	221.7	N.H. 4
	85.9	Mt. Lincoln		220.7	
	86.6	Little Haystack Mountain		220.0	
	88.7	Liberty Spring Tentsite	Cw	217.9	
♦	91.3	Franconia Notch, U.S. 3, Lafayette Place Campground; **North Woodstock, N.H., P.O. 03262** (P.O.,G,L,M 5.8m E; G,L,M 2.2m E; C 2.1m W; L 1.6m E)	RCGLM	215.3	♦
N.H. 5	94.2	Lonesome Lake Hut (L,M,w on A.T.)	LMw	212.4	N.H. 5
	96.1	Kinsman Pond Campsite	CSw	210.5	
	96.7	North Kinsman Mountain		209.9	
	97.6	South Kinsman Mountain		209.0	
	100.1	Eliza Brook Shelter	Sw	206.5	
	103.0	Mt. Wolf (East Peak)		203.6	
♦	107.6	Kinsman Notch, N.H. 112	R	199.0	♦
N.H. 6	109.2	Beaver Brook Shelter	Sw	197.4	N.H. 6
	111.4	Mt. Moosilauke		195.2	
	116.0	Jeffers Brook Shelter	Sw	190.6	
♦	117.1	N.H. 25; **Glencliff, N.H., P.O. 03238** (P.O. 0.5m E)	R	189.5	♦
N.H. 7	119.6	Mt. Mist		187.0	N.H. 7
	122.1	N.H. 25C; **Warren, N.H., P.O. 03279** (w on A.T.; P.O.,G,M 4m E)	RGMw	184.5	
	125.1	Atwell Hill Road	R	181.5	
♦	126.9	N.H. 25A; **Wentworth, N.H., P.O. 03282** (P.O.,G 4.3m E; M 4m W)	RGM	179.7	♦
	130.2	Side trail to Mt. Cube (North Summit)		176.4	

G B S	North to South	FEATURES	Facilities (See page xv for codes)	South to North	G B S
	Miles from Maine-N.H. Line			*Miles from Vt.-Mass. Line*	
	131.8	Hexacuba Shelter (S,w 0.3m E)	Sw	174.8	
N.H. 8	133.3	South Jacob's Brook	w	173.3	N.H. 8
	137.1	Firewarden's Cabin	Sw	169.5	
	137.2	Smarts Mountain Tentsite	Cw	169.4	
	140.9	Lyme-Dorchester Road	Rw	165.7	
◆	142.9	Dartmouth Skiway; **Lyme Center, N.H., P.O. 03769** (P.O. 1.2m W; G,L,M 3.2m W)	RGLM	163.7	◆
	143.8	Trapper John Shelter (S,w 0.2m W)	Sw	162.8	
	144.3	Holts Ledge		162.3	
	146.3	Goose Pond Road	R	160.3	
	147.6	South Fork Hewes Brook	w	159.0	
	149.5	Moose Mountain Shelter (S,w 0.4m E)	Sw	157.1	
	150.0	Moose Mountain (South Peak)		156.6	
N.H. 9	151.6	Mink Brook	w	155.0	N.H. 9
	151.8	Three Mile Road	R	154.8	
	154.3	Etna-Hanover Center Road; **Etna, N.H., P.O. 03750** (P.O. 1.2m E)	R	152.3	
	155.6	Trescott Road	R	151.0	
	158.1	Ledyard Spring (w 0.2m W)	w	148.5	
	158.6	Velvet Rocks Shelter (S 0.2m W)	S	148.0	
	159.4	N.H. 120	R	147.2	
	160.1	Dartmouth College; **Hanover, N.H., P.O. 03755** (P.O.,G,L,M on A.T.)	RGLM	146.5	
◆	160.6	New Hampshire-Vermont Line, Connecticut River	R	146.0	◆

NEW HAMPSHIRE-VERMONT

G B S	North to South	FEATURES	Facilities (See page xv for codes)	South to North	G B S
	Miles from Maine-N.H. Line		*Miles from Vt.-Mass. Line*		
	161.6	**Norwich, Vt., P.O. 05055**			
		(P.O.,G,L,M 0.5m W)	RGLM	145.0	
Vt 1	165.9	Happy Hill Cabin	Sw	140.7	Vt 1
	168.3	Podunk Brook, Podunk Road	Rw	138.3	
	169.1	Tigertown Road, Podunk Road	R	137.5	
◆	169.7	Vt. 14, White River;			◆
		West Hartford, Vt., P.O. 05084			
		(G,M,w on A.T.; P.O. 0.2m E)	RGMw	136.9	
	173.0	Joe Ranger Road	R	133.6	
	174.4	Thistle Hill Shelter	Sw	132.2	
Vt 2	174.8	Thistle Hill		131.8	Vt 2
	176.8	Cloudland Road	R	129.8	
	178.6	South Pomfret-Pomfret Road	Rw	128.0	
	180.8	Woodstock Stage (Barnard Brook) Road;			
		South Pomfret, Vt., P.O. 05067			
		(w on A.T.; P.O.,G 1m E)	RGw	125.8	
◆	182.3	Vt. 12; **Woodstock, Vt., P.O. 05091**			◆
		(P.O.,G,L,M 4.4m E)	RGLM	124.3	
	186.2	Wintturi Shelter			
		(S,w 0.2m W)	Sw	120.4	
	188.7	Side Trail to The Lookout		117.9	
	191.5	Chateauguay Road		115.1	
Vt 3	196.0	Stony Brook Shelter	Sw	110.6	Vt 3
	200.0	River Road	R	106.6	
	200.8	Thundering Brook Road, Kent Pond			
		(L,M,w on A.T.)	RLMw	105.8	
	201.6	Vt. 100, Gifford Woods State Park	RCSw	105.0	
	203.0	Junction with Long Trail,			
		Tucker-Johnson Shelter			
		(S,w 1.3m W)	Sw	103.6	
◆	203.6	Sherburne Pass, U.S. 4, Inn at Long Trail;			◆
		Killington, Vt., P.O. 05751			
		(P.O. 1.2m E; L,M on A.T.; G 1.6m E)	RGLM	103.0	

G B S	North to South	FEATURES	Facilities (See page xv for codes)	South to North	G B S
	Miles from Maine-N.H. Line			*Miles from Vt.-Mass. Line*	
	206.1	Pico Camp	Sw	100.5	
	209.0	Cooper Lodge, Killington Peak Trail (S,w on A.T.; M 0.2m E)	MSw	97.6	
	213.1	Governor Clement Shelter	Sw	93.5	
Vt. 4	214.5	Upper Cold River Road	Rw	92.1	Vt. 4
	215.2	Gould Brook		91.4	
	216.1	Cold River Road (Lower Road)	R	90.5	
	218.4	Lottery Road	R	88.2	
	218.8	Beacon Hill		87.8	
	219.3	Clarendon Shelter	Sw	87.3	
♦	220.5	Vt. 103, **North Clarendon, Vt., P.O. 05759** (P.O.,G,L 4.2m W; M 0.5m W; G 1m W; L 3m W)	RGLM	86.1	♦
	220.6	Clarendon Gorge, Mill River Bridge	w	86.0	
	223.2	Minerva Hinchey Shelter	Sw	83.4	
	224.8	Brook	w	81.8	
	225.8	Vt. 140; **Wallingford, Vt., P.O. 05773** (w on A.T.; P.O.,G,L,M 3.5m W; G 3m E)	RGLMw	80.8	
Vt. 5	226.8	Sugar Hill Road	R	79.8	Vt. 5
	227.7	Greenwall Shelter	Sw	78.9	
	228.5	Trail to White Rocks Cliff		78.1	
	228.8	Spring	w	77.8	
	232.4	Little Rock Pond Shelter	S	74.2	
	232.5	Homer Stone Brook Trail (G 3m W)	G	74.1	
	232.8	Spring	w	73.8	
	232.9	Little Rock Pond Tenting Area	Cw	73.7	
	233.1	Lula Tye Shelter	S	73.5	
♦	234.9	Danby-Landgrove Road (USFS 10), Black Branch; **Danby, Vt., P.O. 05739** (P.O.,G,L,M 3.5m W)	RGLM	71.7	♦

NEW HAMPSHIRE-VERMONT

G B S	North to South	FEATURES	Facilities (See page xv for codes)	South to North	G B S
	Miles from Maine-N.H. Line			*Miles from Vt.-Mass. Line*	
	236.2	Big Branch Shelter	Sw	70.4	
	236.4	Old Job Trail to Old Job Shelter (S,w 1m E)	Sw	70.2	
	237.9	Lost Pond Shelter	Sw	68.7	
	239.9	Baker Peak		66.7	
	241.8	Griffith Lake (north end)	w	64.8	
	242.0	Griffith Lake Tenting Area	Cw	64.6	
Vt. 6	242.5	Peru Peak Shelter	Sw	64.1	**Vt. 6**
	243.8	Peru Peak		62.8	
	245.5	Styles Peak		61.1	
	246.9	Mad Tom Notch, USFS 21; **Peru, Vt., P.O. 05152** (P.O.,G 4.3m E; C 2.5m E)	RCGw	59.7	
	248.6	Mad Tom Shelter	Sw	58.0	
	249.4	Bromley Mountain		57.2	
	251.4	Bromley Tenting Area	Cw	55.2	
◆	252.2	Vt. 11 & 30; **Manchester Center, Vt., P.O. 05255** (P.O.,G,L,M 5.5m W; G 2.5m E; L,M 0.6m E)	RGLM	54.4	◆
	254.5	Spruce Peak		52.1	
	254.9	Spruce Peak Shelter	Sw	51.7	
	257.0	Old Rootville Road, Prospect Rock		49.6	
	258.0	Branch Pond Trail to William B. Douglas Shelter (S,w 0.5m W)	Sw	48.6	
Vt. 7	260.8	Winhall River	w	45.8	**Vt. 7**
	262.6	Stratton Pond, North Shore Trail to North Shore Tenting Area (w on A.T.; C,w 0.5m W)	Cw	44.0	
	262.7	Lye Brook Trail to Bigelow Shelter, Vondell Shelter (w on A.T.; S,w 0.1m W; S 0.2m W)	Sw	43.9	

G B S	North to South	FEATURES	Facilities (See page xv for codes)	South to North	G B S
	Miles from Maine-N.H. Line			*Miles from Vt.-Mass. Line*	
	265.9	Stratton Mountain		40.7	
◆	269.7	Arlington-West Wardsboro Road			◆
		(Kelley Stand Road)	Rw	36.9	
	273.3	Story Spring Shelter	Sw	33.3	
	274.2	South Alder Brook	w	32.4	
	277.9	Caughnawaga and Kid Gore Shelters	Sw	28.7	
Vt 8	281.9	Glastenbury Mountain		24.7	Vt 8
	282.2	Goddard Shelter	Sw	24.4	
	284.7	Glastenbury Lookout		21.9	
	286.5	Little Pond Lookout		20.1	
	289.1	Hell Hollow Brook	w	17.5	
	290.7	Melville Nauheim Shelter	Sw	15.9	
	292.2	City Stream	w	14.4	
◆	292.3	Bennington-Brattleboro Highway (Vt. 9); **Bennington, Vt., P.O. 05201** (P.O.,G,L,M 5.1m W; L 2.4m W, 2.7m E; G 3.9m W)	RGLM	14.3	◆
	294.1	Harmon Hill		12.5	
	296.6	Congdon Camp	Sw	10.0	
Vt 9	300.8	Roaring Branch	w	5.8	Vt 9
	303.5	Mill Road	R	3.1	
	303.8	Seth Warner Shelter and Primitive Camping Area (C,S,w 0.2m W)	CSw	2.8	
	306.2	Brook	w	0.4	
	306.6	Vermont-Massachusetts Line, south end of Long Trail		0.0	

Massachusetts-Connecticut

G B S	North to South	FEATURES	Facilities (See page xv for codes)	South to North	G B S
	Miles from Vt.-Mass. Line			*Miles from Conn.-N.Y. Line*	
◆	0.0	Vermont-Massachusetts Line, south end of Long Trail		141.8	◆
Mass. 1	0.8	Eph's Lookout		141.0	Mass. 1
	1.3	Pine Cobble Trail		140.5	
	2.3	Sherman Brook Campsite	Cw	139.5	
◆	4.1	Mass. 2; **North Adams, Mass., P.O. 01247; Williamstown, Mass., P.O. 01267** (P.O.,G,L,M 2.5m E, 2.6m W; G,M 0.7m E; G,L,M 0.5m W)	RGLM	137.7	◆
	5.0	Pattison Road	Rw	136.8	
	7.1	Wilbur Clearing Lean-to (C,S,w 0.3m W)	CSw	134.7	
Mass. 2	7.2	Notch Road	Rw	134.6	Mass. 2
	10.4	Mt. Greylock, Summit Road, Bascom Lodge (L,M,w on A.T.)	RLMw	131.4	
	10.9	Notch Road, Rockwell Road	R	130.9	
	13.1	Side trail to Jones Nose		128.7	
	13.7	Mark Noepel Lean-to (C,S,w 0.2m E)	CSw	128.1	
	14.6	Old Adams Road		127.2	
	17.3	Outlook Avenue	R	124.5	
◆	18.1	Mass. 8; **Cheshire, Mass., P.O. 01225** (P.O.,L on A.T.; G,M 0.5m W)	RGLM	123.7	◆
	18.7	Hoosic River	R	123.1	
Mass. 3	19.9	The Cobbles		121.9	Mass. 3
	22.3	Gore Pond		119.5	
	22.7	Crystal Mountain Campsite (C,w 0.2m E)	Cw	119.1	
	26.4	Gulf Road		115.4	
◆	27.4	Mass. 8, Mass. 9; **Dalton, Mass., P.O. 01226** (M on A.T.; P.O.,G,L,M 0.3m W)	RGLM	114.4	◆

G B S	North to South	FEATURES	Facilities (See page xv for codes)	South to North	G B S
	Miles from Vt.-Mass. Line			*Miles from Conn.-N.Y. Line*	
	28.0	Conrail		113.8	
	30.1	Grange Hall Road	R	111.7	
Mass. 4	30.4	Kay Wood Lean-to (S,w 0.2m E)	Sw	111.4	**Mass. 4**
	33.1	Warner Hill		108.7	
	33.8	Blotz Road	R	108.0	
	35.0	Stream	w	106.8	
◆	37.0	Pittsfield Road (Washington Mountain Road); **Becket, Mass., P.O. 01223** (P.O.,G,L 5m E; M 1.8m E)	RGLM	104.8	◆
	38.5	West Branch Road	R	103.3	
Mass. 5	39.2	October Mountain Lean-to	CSw	102.6	**Mass. 5**
	40.8	Bald Top Mountain		101.0	
	41.0	County Road	R	100.8	
	43.4	Finerty Pond	w	98.4	
	45.1	Becket Mountain		96.7	
	45.7	Tyne Road	R	96.1	
◆	46.4	U.S. 20; **Lee, Mass., P.O. 01238** (P.O.,G,L,M 5m W; L 0.2m E; M 0.3m W)	RGLM	95.4	◆
	46.7	Stream	w	95.1	
Mass. 6	46.8	Massachusetts Turnpike		95.0	**Mass. 6**
	48.0	Upper Goose Pond Cabin (C,S,w 0.5m W)	CSw	93.8	
	48.8	Upper Goose Pond		93.0	
	50.7	Goose Pond Road	R	91.1	
	53.1	Webster Road	Rw	88.7	
◆	55.0	Main Road; **Tyringham, Mass., P.O. 01264** (P.O.,L 0.9m W)	RL	86.8	◆
Mass. 7	56.1	Jerusalem Road	R	85.7	**Mass. 7**
	57.9	Shaker Campsite	C	83.9	
	58.2	Fernside Road	Rw	83.6	

MASSACHUSETTS-CONNECTICUT

G B S	North to South	FEATURES	Facilities (See page xv for codes)	South to North	G B S
	Miles from Vt.-Mass. Line			*Miles from Conn.-N.Y. Line*	
	61.3	Beartown Mountain Road	w	80.5	
	62.0	Mt. Wilcox North Lean-to			
Mass. 7		(S,w 0.3m E)	Sw	79.8	Mass. 7
	63.8	Mt. Wilcox South Lean-to	Sw	78.0	
	64.5	The Ledges		77.3	
	65.0	Benedict Pond			
		(C,w 0.5m w)	RCw	76.8	
	65.9	Blue Hill Road	R	75.9	
♦	67.1	Mass. 23;			♦
		Great Barrington, Mass., P.O. 01230			
		(P.O.,G,L,M 4m W;			
Mass. 8		L 0.1m E; L,M 2.7m W)	RGLM	74.7	Mass. 8
	69.1	Ice Gulch, Tom Leonard Lean-to	Sw	72.7	
	71.2	East Mountain	w	70.6	
	72.6	Homes Road	R	69.2	
	74.6	Housatonic River	R	67.2	
♦	75.5	U.S. 7;			♦
		Sheffield, Mass., P.O. 01257			
Mass. 9		(P.O.,G,L,M 3.2m E; M 0.1m W, 0.8m E)	RGLM	66.3	Mass. 9
	77.3	South Egremont Road	R	64.5	
	79.1	Mass. 41;			
		South Egremont, Mass., P.O. 01258			
		(P.O.,G,L,M 1.2m W)	RGLM	62.7	
♦	80.0	Jug End Road	Rw	61.8	♦
	81.1	Jug End		60.7	
	82.8	Elbow Trail		59.0	
Mass. 10	83.4	Glen Brook Lean-to	Sw	58.4	Mass. 10
	83.9	Guilder Pond Picnic Area	R	57.9	
	84.6	Mt. Everett	R	57.2	
	85.3	Race Brook Trail			
		(C,w 0.4m E)	Cw	56.5	
	86.4	Race Mountain		55.4	
	88.1	Bear Rock Stream Campsite	Cw	53.7	

MASSACHUSETTS-CONNECTICUT

G B S	North to South	FEATURES	Facilities (See page xv for codes)	South to North	G B S
	Miles from Vt.-Mass. Line			*Miles from Conn.-N.Y. Line*	
◆	89.5	Sages Ravine	w	52.3	◆
	90.0	Campsites	Cw	51.8	
	90.4	Massachusetts-Connecticut Line		51.4	
	90.9	Bear Mountain		50.9	
	91.6	Bear Mountain Road		50.2	
	91.8	Riga Junction, Undermountain Trail		50.0	
Conn. 1	92.3	Brassie Brook (South Branch), Brassie Brook Lean-to	CSw	49.5	Conn. 1
	92.9	Ball Brook	Cw	48.9	
	93.5	Riga Lean-to	CSw	48.3	
	94.2	Lions Head		47.6	
	96.7	Plateau Campsite	Cw	45.1	
◆	96.9	Conn. 41 (Undermountain Road); **Salisbury, Conn., P.O. 06068** (P.O.,G,L,M 0.8m W)	RGLM	44.9	◆
	97.6	U.S. 44	R	44.2	
	100.1	Billy's View		41.7	
	100.9	Rand's View		40.9	
Conn. 2	101.0	Side trail to Limestone Spring Lean-to (C,S,w 0.5m W)	CSw	40.8	Conn. 2
	101.7	Prospect Mountain		40.1	
	104.0	Spring	w	37.8	
	104.5	Housatonic River Road	R	37.3	
	105.0	Iron Bridge over Housatonic River; **Falls Village, Conn., P.O. 06031** (P.O.,M 0.5m E)	RM	36.8	
	106.8	Mohawk Trail (L,M 0.2m E)	LM	35.0	
◆	107.0	U.S. 7, Housatonic River	R	34.8	◆
	107.7	U.S. 7, Conn. 112	R	34.1	
Conn. 3	108.1	Belter Campsite	Cw	33.7	Conn. 3
	110.9	Sharon Mountain Campsite	Cw	30.9	
	112.1	Mt. Easter		29.7	

MASSACHUSETTS-CONNECTICUT

G B S	North to South	FEATURES	Facilities (See page xv for codes)	South to North	G B S
	Miles from Vt.-Mass. Line			*Miles from Conn.-N.Y. Line*	
	112.4	State Forest Road	R	29.4	
	113.3	Pine Swamp Brook Lean-to	Sw	28.5	
Conn. 3	114.4	West Cornwall Road; **West Cornwall, Conn., P.O. 06796** (P.O.,G 2.2m E)	RG	27.4	Conn. 3
	114.5	Carse Brook	w	27.3	
	116.7	Caesar Road	C	25.1	
	117.2	Pine Knob Loop Trail		24.6	
	117.8	Hatch Brook		24.0	
	119.0	Old Sharon Road	R	22.8	
◆	119.2	Conn. 4; **Cornwall Bridge, Conn., P.O. 06754** (P.O.,G,L 0.9m E)	RGL	22.6	◆
	120.1	Silver Hill Campsite	Cw	21.7	
	120.9	River Road	Rw	20.9	
Conn. 4	122.9	Stony Brook Campsite	Cw	18.9	Conn. 4
	123.3	Stewart Hollow Brook Lean-to	CSw	18.5	
	125.6	River Road	R	16.2	
	126.1	St. Johns Ledges		15.7	
	126.8	Caleb's Peak		15.0	
	127.5	Skiff Mountain Road	R	14.3	
◆	130.3	Conn. 341, Schaghticoke Road; **Kent, Conn., P.O. 06757** (P.O.,G,L,M 0.8m E)	RGLM	11.5	◆
	130.6	Mt. Algo Lean-to	CSw	11.2	
	131.6	Thayer Brook		10.2	
Conn. 5	133.5	Schaghticoke Mountain Campsite	Cw	8.3	Conn. 5
	134.1	Indian Rocks		7.7	
	134.6	Connecticut-New York Line		7.2	
	135.7	Schaghticoke Mountain		6.1	
	137.4	Schaghticoke Road	R	4.4	
	137.9	Bulls Bridge Road Parking Area (G,M 0.2m E)	RGM	3.9	

G B S	North to South	FEATURES	Facilities (See page xv for codes)	South to North	G B S
	Miles from Vt.-Mass. Line			*Miles from Conn.-N.Y. Line*	
Conn. 5	138.8	Ten Mile River	Cw	3.0	Conn. 5
	139.0	Ten Mile River Lean-to	S	2.8	
	140.0	Ten Mile Hill		1.8	
	141.1	Conn. 55	R	0.7	
	141.8	Hoyt Road, Connecticut-New York Line; Wingdale, N.Y., P.O. 12594 (P.O.,G,M 3.3m W; M 1.5m W, 2.3m W)	RGM	0.0	

New York-New Jersey

G B S	North to South	FEATURES	Facilities (See page xv for codes)	South to North	G B S
	Miles from Conn.-N.Y. Line			*Miles from Delaware Water Gap, Pa.*	
◆	0.0	Hoyt Road, Connecticut-New York Line; **Wingdale, N.Y., P.O. 12594** (P.O.,G,M 3.3m W;			◆
N.Y. 2		M 1.5m W, 2.3m W)	RGM	161.8	N.Y. 2
	1.0	Duell Hollow Road	R	160.8	
	1.2	Wiley Shelter	Sw	160.6	
	1.6	Leather Hill Road	R	160.2	
	6.9	Hurds Corners Road	R	154.9	
◆	7.1	N.Y. 22, Metro-North Railroad, Appalachian Trail R.R. Station (G 0.6m E; L 2.6m W)	RGL	154.7	◆
N.Y. 3	9.5	County 20 (West Dover Road); **Pawling, N.Y., P.O. 12564** (P.O.,G,M 2.9m E; C 3.1m E; G 3.2m E; L 4m E))	RCGLM	152.3	N.Y. 3
	10.2	Telephone Pioneers Shelter	Sw	151.6	
	10.5	West Mountain		151.3	
◆	14.1	N.Y. 55; **Poughquag, N.Y., P.O. 12570** (P.O.,M 3.1m W; G,M 1.5m W; L 2.1m W)	RGLM	147.7	◆
N.Y. 4	14.4	Old Route 55	R	147.4	N.Y. 4
	16.3	Depot Hill Road	R	145.5	
	17.4	Morgan Stewart Shelter	Sw	144.4	
	17.5	Mt. Egbert		144.3	
	19.9	Stormville Mountain Road, I-84	R	141.9	
◆	21.3	N.Y. 52; **Stormville, N.Y., P.O. 12582** (P.O. 1.9m W; G 0.4m E, 2.2m W;			◆
N.Y. 5		M 2m E; G,M 2.4m W)	RGM	140.5	N.Y. 5
	22.9	Hosner Mountain Road	R	138.9	
◆	26.1	Taconic State Parkway	R	135.7	◆
N.Y. 6	26.4	Hortontown Road, RPH Shelter (S,w on A.T.; G 1.2m W)	RGSw	135.4	N.Y. 6
	28.8	Long Hill Road	R	133.0	

NEW YORK-NEW JERSEY

G B S	North to South	FEATURES	Facilities (See page xv for codes)	South to North	G B S
	Miles from Conn.-N.Y. Line			*Miles from Delaware Water Gap, Pa.*	
◆	29.2	Shenandoah Mountain		132.6	
◆	33.3	N.Y. 301, Canopus Lake, Fahnestock State Park			◆
N.Y. 7		(C,w 1m E)	RCw	128.5	N.Y. 7
	35.4	Sunk Mine Road	R	126.4	
	36.9	Dennytown Road	RCw	124.9	
	39.7	South Highland Road	R	122.1	
◆	40.7	Canopus Hill Road	R	121.1	◆
N.Y. 8	42.4	Old Albany Post Road, Chapman Road	R	119.4	N.Y. 8
	43.2	Denning Hill		118.6	
	45.1	Old West Point Road, Graymoor Monastery	R	116.7	
◆	45.7	U.S. 9, N.Y. 403; **Peekskill, N.Y., P.O. 10566** (P.O.,G,L,M 4.5m E;			◆
N.Y. 9		G 1.9m E)	RGLM	116.1	N.Y. 9
	49.1	South Mountain Pass (Manitou Road)	R	112.7	
	49.3	Hemlock Springs Campsite	Cw	112.5	
	50.3	Camp Smith Trail, Anthony's Nose		111.5	
	50.8	N.Y. 9D	R	111.0	
◆	51.5	Bear Mountain Bridge; **Fort Montgomery, N.Y., P.O. 10922** (P.O.,G,L,M 0.7m W)	RGLM	110.3	◆
	51.6	Trailside Museum and Zoo		110.2	
	52.3	Bear Mountain Inn, **Bear Mountain, N.Y., P.O. 10911**			
N.Y. 10		(P.O. 0.3m E; L,M,w on A.T.)	RLMw	109.5	N.Y. 10
	54.1	Bear Mountain	Rw	107.7	
	55.7	Seven Lakes Drive	R	106.1	
	57.3	Trail to West Mountain Shelter (S 0.6m E)	S(nw)	104.5	
	58.2	Beechy Bottom Brook	w	103.6	
	58.5	Palisades Interstate Parkway	R	103.3	
	59.2	Black Mountain		102.6	

NEW YORK-NEW JERSEY

	Miles from Conn.-N.Y. Line			*Miles from Delaware Water Gap, Pa.*	
N.Y. 10	60.6	William Brien Memorial Shelter	S(nw)	101.2	N.Y. 10
	61.8	Goshen Mountain		100.0	
	62.6	Seven Lakes Drive	R	99.2	
♦	64.8	Arden Valley Road			♦
		(w 0.3m E)	Rw	97.0	
	65.9	Fingerboard Shelter	S(nw)	95.9	
N.Y. 11	66.9	Surebridge Mountain		94.9	N.Y. 11
	68.0	Lemon Squeezer		93.8	
	68.6	Island Pond Outlet	w	93.2	
	69.9	Arden Valley Road	R	91.9	
	70.1	New York State Thruway		91.7	
♦	70.3	N.Y. 17; **Arden, N.Y., P.O. 10910; Southfields, N.Y., P.O. 10975** (P.O. 0.7m W; P.O.,L,M 2.1m E; G 1.8m E, 5.7m E)	RGLM	91.5	♦
	71.4	Arden Mountain		90.4	
	72.1	Orange Turnpike (w 0.5m E)	Rw	89.7	
	72.8	Little Dam Lake		89.0	
N.Y. 12	73.5	East Mombasha Road	R	88.3	N.Y. 12
	74.3	Buchanan Mountain		87.5	
	75.2	West Mombasha Road (G 0.6m W)	RG	86.6	
	76.4	Mombasha High Point		85.4	
	78.4	Fitzgerald Falls	w	83.4	
	78.7	Lakes Road	R	83.1	
	80.2	Wildcat Shelter	Sw	81.6	
	80.5	Cat Rocks		81.3	
	81.0	Eastern Pinnacles		80.8	
♦ N.Y. 13	82.3	N.Y. 17A; **Bellvale, N.Y., P.O. 10912; Greenwood Lake, N.Y., P.O. 10925** (P.O.,G 1.6m W; P.O.,G,L,M 2m E G,L,M 3.5m W)	RGLM	79.5	♦ N.Y. 13

G B S	North to South	FEATURES	Facilities (See page xv for codes)	South to North	G B S
	Miles from Conn.-N.Y. Line			*Miles from Delaware Water Gap, Pa.*	
	87.7	Prospect Rock		74.1	
♦	88.2	State Line Trail, New York-New Jersey Line			♦
		(L 3m E; M 2.3m E)	LM	73.6	
	89.3	Long House Creek		72.5	
	90.4	Long House Road (Brady Road)			
		(G,M 0.7m W)	RGM	71.4	
	91.8	Warwick Turnpike			
		(G 1.8m E; L 0.8m W; M 1.5m E)	RGLM	70.0	
N.J. 1	92.2	Wawayanda Shelter			N.J. 1
		(S on A.T.; w 0.4m E)	Sw	69.6	
	92.4	Wawayanda Road	R	69.4	
	93.3	Iron Mountain Road Bridge		68.5	
	94.5	Barrett Road;			
		New Milford, N.Y., P.O. 10959			
		(P.O.,G 1.8m W)	RG	67.3	
	96.4	Wawayanda Mountain		65.4	
♦	97.8	N.J. 94; **Vernon, N.J., P.O. 07462**			♦
		(P.O.,G,M 2.4m E; L 1.5m E)	RGLM	64.0	
	98.7	Canal Road	R	63.1	
	100.0	County 517;			
		Glenwood, N.J., P.O. 07418			
N.J. 2		(P.O.,G,L 1.1m W)	RGL	61.8	N.J. 2
	102.4	County 565	R	59.4	
	103.6	Pochuck Mountain		58.2	
	105.2	Pochuck Mountain Shelter	S(ʀw)	56.6	
	105.6	Wallkill Road (Liberty Corners Road)	Rw	56.2	
	107.9	Wallkill River	R	53.9	
	108.9	Oil City Road	R	52.9	
♦	109.4	N.J. 284			♦
		(G 0.4m W)	RG	52.4	
N.J. 3	110.4	Lott Road; **Unionville, N.Y., P.O. 10988**			N.J. 3
		(P.O.,G,M 0.4m W)	RGM	51.4	

NEW YORK-NEW JERSEY

G B S	North to South	FEATURES	Facilities (See page xv for codes)	South to North	G B S
	Miles from Conn.-N.Y. Line			*Miles from Delaware Water Gap, Pa.*	
N.J. 3	111.4	Unionville Road	R	50.4	**N.J. 3**
	113.7	Gemmer Road	R	48.1	
	116.3	County 519	R	45.5	
	117.6	High Point Shelter	Sw	44.2	
	118.1	Side trail to High Point Monument		43.7	
♦	119.3	N.J. 23 (w on A.T.; G 2.5m E, 4.3m W; L 1.4m E, 4.4m W; M 4.3m W)	RGLMw	42.5	♦
	121.8	Trail to Rutherford Shelter (S,w 0.4m E)	Sw	40.0	
N.J. 4	124.6	Deckertown Turnpike	Rw	37.2	**N.J. 4**
	124.8	Mashipacong Shelter	S	37.0	
	127.3	Crigger Road		34.5	
	128.2	Sunrise Mountain	R	33.6	
	130.5	Trail to Gren Anderson Shelter (S,w 0.3m W)	Sw	31.3	
	131.6	Culver Fire Tower		30.2	
♦	133.6	Culvers Gap, U.S. 206; **Branchville, N.J., P.O. 07826** (P.O. 3.4m E; G on A.T., 1.6m E; L 2.5m E, 1.9m W; M 0.1m W, 0.6m E)	RGLM	28.2	♦
N.J. 5	137.3	Brink Road Shelter (S,w 0.2m W)	Sw	24.5	**N.J. 5**
	139.6	Rattlesnake Mountain		22.2	
	141.4	Buttermilk Falls Trail		20.4	
	144.4	Flatbrookville Road	Rw	17.4	
♦	148.2	Millbrook-Blairstown Road	R	13.6	♦
	148.6	Rattlesnake Spring	w	13.2	
N.J. 6	149.2	Catfish Fire Tower		12.6	**N.J. 6**
	151.5	Camp Road (L,w 0.5m W)	RLw	10.3	

G B S	North to South	FEATURES	Facilities (See page xv for codes)	South to North	G B S
	Miles from Conn.-N.Y. Line			*Miles from Delaware Water Gap, Pa.*	
	155.8	Spring	w	6.0	
	155.9	Sunfish Pond		5.9	
	157.2	Backpacker Site	C(nw)	4.6	
N.J. 6	158.8	Trail to Holly Spring (w 0.2m E)	w	3.0	N.J. 6
	160.4	I-80 Overpass	R	1.4	
	160.8	Delaware Water Gap National Recreation Area Information Center	Rw	1.0	
	161.8	Delaware River Bridge (west end)	R	0.0	

Pennsylvania

G B S	North to South	FEATURES	Facilities (See page xv for codes)	South to North	G B S
	Miles from Delaware Water Gap, Pa.			*Miles from Pa.-Md. Line*	
◆	0.0	Delaware River Bridge (west end)	R	232.0	◆
	0.2	Pa. 611, **Delaware Water Gap, Pa., P.O. 18327** (P.O.,M 0.1m W; L,M 0.4m W; G,L 3.2m W)	RGLM	231.8	
Pa. 1	0.8	Council Rock		231.2	Pa. 1
	1.7	Lookout Rock		230.3	
	2.6	Mt. Minsi		229.4	
	4.7	Totts Gap		227.3	
	6.6	Kirkridge Shelter	Sw	225.4	
	7.2	Fox Gap, Pa. 191	R	224.8	
	8.8	Wolf Rocks		223.2	
◆	15.3	Pa. 33; **Wind Gap, Pa., P.O. 18091** (P.O.,G,L,M 1m E; L 0.1m W)	RGLM	216.7	◆
	16.3	Hahns Lookout		215.7	
	19.9	Leroy A. Smith Shelter (S 0.1m E; w 0.2m E)	Sw	212.1	
	23.3	Smith Gap Road (w 1m W)	Rw	208.7	
Pa. 2	25.9	Delps Trail (w 1m E)	w	206.1	Pa. 2
	30.8	Little Gap; **Danielsville, Pa., P.O. 18038** (P.O.,G,M 1.5m E)	RGM	201.2	
	35.5	Pa. 248	R	196.5	
	35.7	Lehigh River Bridge (east end), Pa. 873; **Palmerton, Pa., P.O. 18071** (P.O.,G,L,M 2m W)	RGLM	196.3	
◆	35.9	Lehigh Gap, Pa. 873; **Slatington, Pa., P.O. 18080** (P.O.,G,L,M 2m E)	RGLM	196.1	◆
Pa. 3	36.5	Spring	w	195.5	Pa. 3
	36.6	George W. Outerbridge Shelter	S	195.4	

G B S	North to South	FEATURES	Facilities (See page xv for codes)	South to North	G B S
	Miles from *Delaware Water Gap, Pa.*			*Miles from* *Pa.-Md. Line*	
	41.0	Ashfield Road, Lehigh Furnace Gap; **Ashfield, Pa., P.O. 18212** (P.O.,G 2.2m W; w 0.7m E)	RGw	191.0	
	44.3	Bake Oven Knob Shelter	Sw	187.7	
Pa. 3	45.0	Bake Oven Knob		187.0	Pa. 3
	45.4	Bake Oven Knob Road	R	186.6	
	46.8	Bear Rocks		185.2	
	47.7	The Cliffs		184.3	
	48.5	New Tripoli Campsite (C,w 0.3m W)	Cw	183.5	
◆	50.3	Pa. 309, Blue Mountain Summit	RM	181.7	◆
	52.5	Jacksonville-Snyders Road	R	179.5	
	54.5	Allentown Hiking Club Shelter	Sw	177.5	
	55.8	Tri-County Corner		176.2	
	63.0	Hawk Mountain Road, Eckville Shelter (S,w 0.2m E)	RSw	169.0	
	68.4	The Pinnacle		163.6	
Pa. 4	68.8	Trail to Blue Rocks Campground (C,G,S 1.5m E)	CGS	163.2	Pa. 4
	70.5	Pulpit Rock		161.5	
	72.4	Windsor Furnace Shelter	Sw	159.6	
	72.7	Windsor Furnace (C,w 0.3m E)	Cw	159.3	
	75.4	Pocahontas Spring (C,w on A.T.; L,M 1m E)	CLMw	156.6	
	78.0	Pa. 61 (M 0.5m W)	RM	154.0	
◆	78.7	**Port Clinton, Pa., P.O. 19549** (P.O. on A.T.; L,S 0.5m W; G,L,M 3m E)	RGLMS	153.3	◆
Pa. 5	83.5	Phillip's Canyon Spring	w	148.5	Pa. 5

PENNSYLVANIA

G B S	North to South	FEATURES	Facilities (See page xv for codes)	South to North	G B S
	Miles from Delaware Water Gap, Pa.			*Miles from Pa.-Md. Line*	
	85.6	Shartlesville Cross-Mountain Road, **Shartlesville, Pa., P.O. 19554** (P.O.,G,L,M 3.6m E)	GLM	146.4	
Pa. 5	87.5	Eagle's Nest Shelter (S,w 0.3m W)	Sw	144.5	Pa. 5
	88.4	Sand Spring Trail (w 0.2m E)	w	143.6	
	92.3	Black Swatara Spring (w 0.3m E)	w	139.7	
♦	93.7	Pa. 183, Rentschler Marker	R	138.3	♦
	94.0	Fort Dietrich Snyder Marker (w 0.2m W)	w	138.0	
	97.4	Shuberts Gap		134.6	
	97.5	Hertlein Campsite	Cw	134.5	
	99.9	Trail to Round Head and Shower Steps	w	132.1	
Pa. 6	101.4	Trail to Pilger Ruh Spring	Cw	130.6	Pa. 6
	101.7	Pa. 501; **Pine Grove, Pa., P.O. 17963,** 501 Shelter (P.O.,M 3.7m W; S,w 0.1m W; G 4.3m W; L 5.7m W)	RGLMSw	130.3	
	103.8	Pa. 645	R	128.2	
	106.2	Blue Mountain Spring, William Penn Shelter	Sw	125.8	
♦	113.6	I-81		118.4	♦
	113.9	Swatara Gap, Pa. 72 (G 2m E)	RG	118.1	
	115.7	Pa. 443; **Green Point, Pa.**	R	116.3	
Pa. 7	117.1	Spring	w	114.9	Pa. 7
	119.6	Rausch Gap Shelter (S,w 0.3m E)	Sw	112.4	
	121.9	Cold Spring Trail		110.1	
	124.2	Yellow Springs Village Site		107.8	

G B S	North to South	FEATURES	Facilities (See page xv for codes)	South to North	G B S
	Miles from Delaware Water Gap, Pa.			*Miles from Pa.-Md. Line*	
	127.5	Stony Mountain; Horse-Shoe Trail		104.5	
◆	130.8	Pa. 325, Clarks Valley	Rw	101.2	◆
	131.2	Spring	w	100.8	
	134.0	Shikellimy Rocks		98.0	
Pa. 8	137.3	Peters Mountain Shelter	Sw	94.7	Pa. 8
	138.3	Table Rock		93.7	
	140.4	Pa. 225	R	91.6	
	144.3	Clarks Ferry Shelter	Sw	87.7	
	147.2	U.S. 22 & 322, Conrail	R	84.8	
◆	147.7	Clarks Ferry Bridge (west end), Susquehanna River (C on A.T.; L,M 0.1m W)	RCLM	84.3	◆
	147.9	Juniata River, Pa. 849	R	84.1	
	148.9	**Duncannon, Pa., P.O. 17020** (P.O.,L,M on A.T., G 0.6m W)	RGLM	83.1	
Pa. 9	149.5	U.S. 11 & 15, Pa. 274	R	82.5	Pa. 9
	151.1	Hawk Rock		80.9	
	153.0	Thelma Marks Memorial Shelter	Sw	79.0	
	158.1	Pa. 850	R	73.9	
	160.3	Darlington Shelter	Sw	71.7	
	160.4	Darlington Trail		71.6	
◆	162.3	Pa. 944; **Donnellytown, Pa.**	R	69.7	◆
	164.3	Conodoguinet Creek (G 0.3m W)	RG	67.7	
	165.7	I-81 Crossing	R	66.3	
Pa. 10	166.6	U.S. 11 (G 1.3m E; L 0.6m E, 0.3m W; M 0.3m E, 0.3m W)	RGLM	65.4	Pa. 10
	167.8	Pennsylvania Turnpike	R	64.2	
	170.5	Trindle Road (Pa. 641)	R	61.5	
	172.6	Pa. 74	R	59.4	

PENNSYLVANIA

G B S	North to South	FEATURES	Facilities (See page xv for codes)	South to North	G B S
	Miles from Delaware Water Gap, Pa.			*Miles from Pa.-Md. Line*	
	211.4	Quarry Gap Shelters	Sw	20.6	
	211.8	Quarry Gap Road	R	20.2	
◆	214.0	U.S. 30, Caledonia State Park, Thaddeus Stevens Museum; **Fayetteville, Pa., P.O. 17222** (P.O.,G,L,M 3.5m W; C,w on A.T.; M 0.5m W; G 0.9m W)	RCGLMw	18.0	◆
	217.0	Rocky Mountain Shelters (S 0.2m E; w 0.5m E)	Sw	15.0	
	218.7	Pa. 233; **South Mountain, Pa., P.O. 17261** (P.O.,G 1.2m E)	RG	13.3	
	219.0	Swamp Road	R	13.0	
	222.3	Chimney Rocks		9.7	
	223.6	Tumbling Run Shelters, Hermitage Cabin (locked)	Sw	8.4	
	223.9	Antietam Road (Old Forge Road)	R	8.1	
	224.4	Rattlesnake Run Road	R	7.6	
	224.8	Antietam Shelter, Old Forge Park	RSw	7.2	
	227.2	Deer Lick Shelters	Sw	4.8	
	228.5	Bailey Spring	w	3.5	
	229.1	Mackie Run, Mentzer Gap Road	R	2.9	
	229.3	Pa. 16; **Blue Ridge Summit, Pa., P.O. 17214** (P.O.,M 2.2m E; M 2m W)	RM	2.7	
	229.6	Old Pa. 16	R	2.4	
	230.8	Buena Vista Road	Rw	1.2	
	231.9	Pen Mar Road	R	0.1	
	232.0	Pennsylvania-Maryland Line	R	0.0	

Pa. 14

Maryland-West Virginia-
Northern Virginia

G B S	North to South	FEATURES	Facilities (See page xv for codes)	South to North	G B S
	Miles from Pa.-Md. Line			*Miles from Front Royal, Va.*	
◆	0.0	Pennsylvania-Maryland Line	R	94.2	◆
	0.2	Pen Mar Park; **Cascade, Md., P.O. 21719** (P.O. 1.6m E; C,w on A.T.;			
Md. 1		G 1.1m E; M 1.4m E)	RCGMw	94.0	Md. 1
	3.1	Trail to High Rock	R	91.1	
	4.9	Devils Racecourse Shelter Trail (C,S,w 0.3m E)	CSw	89.3	
◆	5.8	Raven Rock Hollow, Md. 491, Ritchie Road	R	88.4	◆
Md. 2	6.6	Warner Gap Road	Rw	87.6	Md. 2
	8.0	Foxville Road (Md. 77)	R	86.2	
	9.2	Spring	w	85.0	
◆	9.3	Wolfsville Road (Md. 17); **Smithsburg, Md., P.O. 21783** (P.O.,G,M 2.4m W; L 6.4m W)	RGLM	84.9	◆
	9.4	Hemlock Hill Campground and Shelter	CS	84.8	
Md. 3	13.7	Pogo Memorial Campsite	Cw	80.5	Md. 3
	14.4	Black Rock Cliffs		79.8	
	15.4	Trail to Annapolis Rocks (w 0.2m W)	w	78.8	
	17.1	Pine Knob Shelter	CSw	77.1	
◆	17.6	I-70 Footbridge, U.S. 40 (C 1.4m W; M,w 0.4m W)	RCMw	76.6	◆
Md. 4	18.4	Boonsboro Mountain Road	R	75.8	Md. 4
	20.6	Washington Monument		73.6	
	20.8	Washington Monument State Park	Rw	73.4	
	21.1	Zittlestown Road	R	73.1	

G B S	North to South	FEATURES	Facilities (See page xv for codes)	South to North	G B S
	Miles from Pa.-Md. Line		*Miles from Front Royal, Va.*		
◆	22.6	Turners Gap, U.S. Alt. 40; **Boonsboro, Md., P.O. 21713** (P.O.,M 2.4m W; G 1.7m W, 3.8m W; M 0.1m W)	RGM	71.6	◆
	22.8	Dahlgren Back Pack Campground	Cw	71.4	
	23.6	Reno Monument Road	R	70.6	
Md. 5	24.5	Rocky Run Shelter (C,S,w 0.2m W)	CSw	69.7	Md. 5
	26.1	Lambs Knoll		68.1	
	26.3	White Rock Cliff		67.9	
	26.8	Trail to Bear Spring Cabin (locked) (w 0.3m E)	w	67.4	
	29.4	Crampton Gap Shelter (C,S,w 0.3m E)	CSw	64.8	
◆	29.8	Crampton Gap, Gathland State Park, Gapland Road (Md. 572); **Burkittsville, Md., P.O. 21718** (P.O. 1.2m E; w on A.T.)	Rw	64.4	◆
Md. 6	31.6	Brownsville Gap		62.6	Md. 6
	35.6	Trail to Weverton Cliffs		58.6	
◆	36.5	Weverton	R	57.7	◆
	36.7	U.S. 340 Underpass		57.5	
	37.0	C&O Canal Towpath (east junction)		57.2	
Md. 7	37.3	Weverton Primitive Camp	C(nw)	56.9	Md. 7
	38.5	U.S. 340, Sandy Hook Bridge (G 0.1m W; L 0.4m W; L,M 0.6m W)	RGLM	55.7	
	39.6	C&O Canal Towpath (west junction)		54.6	
◆	39.8	Potomac River, Byron Memorial Footbridge, Maryland-West Virginia Line		54.4	◆

MARYLAND-
WEST VIRGINIA-
NORTHERN VIRGINIA

G B S	North to South	FEATURES	Facilities (See page xv for codes)	South to North	G B S
	Miles from Pa.-Md. Line			*Miles from Front Royal, Va.*	
	39.9	Shenandoah Street; Harpers Ferry National Historical Park (M 0.1m W)	RM	54.3	
W.Va.-Va. 1	40.5	Appalachian Trail Conference Side Trail; **Harpers Ferry, W.Va., P.O. 25425** (P.O. 0.5m W; G 1.1m W; L 0.6m W; M 0.4m W; ATC 0.2m W; C 1.6m W)	RCGLM	53.7	W.Va.-Va. 1
	40.8	U.S. 340, Shenandoah River Bridge (L 0.1m W)	RL	53.4	
	41.5	Chestnut Hill Road (W.Va. 32)	R	52.7	
	42.2	Loudoun Heights, W.Va.-Va. Line		52.0	
◆	46.1	Keys Gap, W.Va. 9 (G,M,w 0.3m W, 0.3m E)	RGMw	48.1	◆
	49.1	David Lesser Memorial Shelter (S 0.1m E; w 0.3m E)	Sw	45.1	
W.Va.-Va. 2	52.3	Trail to Blackburn Trail Center (C 0.1m E; S,w 0.3m E)	CSw	41.9	W.Va.-Va. 2
	53.5	Wilson Gap		40.7	
	56.3	Devils Racecourse		37.9	
	56.4	Sand Spring	w	37.8	
	57.0	Crescent Rock		37.2	
	57.3	Spring	w	36.9	
◆	59.6	Snickers Gap, Va. 7, Va. 679; **Bluemont, Va., P.O. 22012** (P.O. 0.3m E; G 1m W; M 0.3m W, 0.9m W)	RGM	34.6	◆
Va. 3	60.2	Bears Den Rocks, Bears Den Hostel (L,w 0.2m E)	Lw	34.0	Va. 3
	60.5	Spring	w	33.7	
	63.2	Sawmill Spring, Sam Moore Shelter	Sw	31.0	

G B S	North to South	FEATURES	Facilities (See page xv for codes)	South to North	G B S
	Miles from Pa.-Md. Line			*Miles from Front Royal, Va.*	
Va. 3	65.2	Spring	w	29.0	Va. 3
	66.4	Va. 605	R	27.8	
◆	70.1	Rod Hollow Shelter	Sw	24.1	◆
	73.7	Ashby Gap, U.S. 50			
		(G 0.2m E; M 0.8m W; L,M 1.2m E)	RGLM	20.5	
	76.8	Sky Meadows State Park Side Trail			
		(C,S,w 1.3m E)	CSw	17.4	
Va. 4	78.1	Spring	w	16.1	Va. 4
	79.1	Dick's Dome Shelter			
		(S,w 0.2m E)	Sw	15.1	
	81.6	Trico Trail		12.6	
	83.5	Manassas Gap Shelter	Sw	10.7	
◆	86.0	Va. 55; **Linden, Va., P.O. 22642**			◆
		(P.O.,G 1m W)	RG	8.2	
	87.9	Va. 638	R	6.3	
Va. 5	89.0	Jim & Molly Denton Shelter	CSw	5.2	Va. 5
	90.9	Tom Sealock Spring	w	3.3	
	94.2	U.S. 522; **Front Royal, Va., P.O. 22630**			
		(P.O.,G 4.2m W; G,M 3.2m W; L,M 3.6m W)	RGLM	0.0	

Shenandoah National Park

G B S	North to South	FEATURES	Facilities (See page xv for codes)	South to North	G B S
	Miles from Front Royal, Va.			*Miles from Rockfish Gap, Va.*	
◆	0.0	U.S. 522; **Front Royal, Va., P.O. 22630** (P.O.,G 4.2m W; G,M 3.2m W; L,M 3.6m W)	RGLM	106.9	◆
	1.4	Va. 602	R	105.5	
	2.9	Tom Floyd Wayside; self-registration station for SNP camping permits	Sw	104.0	
	3.6	Possum's Rest Overlook; northern boundary, Shenandoah National Park		103.3	
	3.9	Compton Gap Fire Road		103.0	
SNP 1	5.4	Indian Run Spring (w 0.3m E)	w	101.5	SNP 1
	5.7	Compton Gap; Skyline Drive, mile 10.4	R	101.2	
	6.5	Compton Peak		100.4	
	6.9	Compton Springs	w	100.0	
	7.7	Jenkins Gap; Skyline Drive, mile 12.3	R	99.2	
	9.4	Hogwallow Gap; Skyline Drive, mile 14.2	R	97.5	
	10.0	Hogwallow Spring	w	96.9	
	10.9	North Marshall Mountain		96.0	
	11.5	Skyline Drive, mile 15.9	R	95.4	
	12.1	South Marshall Mountain		94.8	
◆	13.1	Gravel Springs Gap; Skyline Drive, mile 17.7	R	93.8	◆
	13.3	Gravel Springs Hut (S,w 0.2m E)	Sw	93.6	
SNP 2	14.4	Skyline Drive, mile 18.9	R	92.5	SNP 2
	14.9	Little Hogback Mountain		92.0	
	15.0	Little Hogback Overlook; Skyline Drive, mile 19.7	R	91.9	
	15.7	First peak of Hogback		91.2	
	15.8	Spring (w 0.2m E)	w	91.1	

SHENANDOAH NATIONAL PARK

G B S	North to South	FEATURES	Facilities (See page xv for codes)	South to North	G B S
	Miles from Front Royal, Va.			*Miles from Rockfish Gap, Va.*	
	16.0	Second peak of Hogback		90.9	
	16.2	Skyline Drive, mile 20.8	R	90.7	
	16.3	Third Peak of Hogback		90.6	
	16.5	Skyline Drive, mile 21.1	R	90.4	
	16.9	Tuscarora Trail		90.0	
	17.5	Rattlesnake Point Overlook; Skyline Drive, mile 21.9	R	89.4	
SNP 2	18.2	Range View Cabin (locked) (0.1m E)	w	88.7	SNP 2
	19.0	Elkwallow Gap; Skyline Drive, mile 23.9 (G,M 0.1m E)	RGM	87.9	
	19.5	Spring	w	87.4	
	24.1	Byrd's Nest #4 Picnic Shelter (0.5m E)	w	82.8	
	24.3	Beahms Gap; Skyline Drive, mile 28.5	R	82.6	
	24.5	Skyline Drive, mile 28.6	R	82.4	
	25.6	Pass Mountain		81.3	
	26.4	Pass Mountain Hut (S,w 0.2m E)	Sw	80.5	
◆	27.6	Thornton Gap, U.S. 211; Skyline Drive, mile 31.5 (G,M on A.T.)	RGM	79.3	◆
	29.3	Marys Rock		77.6	
	30.0	Meadow Spring (w 0.3m E)	w	76.9	
SNP 3	30.6	Byrd's Nest #3 Picnic Shelter		76.3	SNP 3
	31.6	The Pinnacle		75.3	
	32.6	Side trail to Jewell Hollow Overlook; Skyline Drive, mile 36.4	R	74.3	
	32.7	Pinnacles Picnic Ground; Skyline Drive, mile 36.7	Rw	74.2	
	34.9	Hughes River Gap, side trail to Stony Man Mountain Overlook; Skyline Drive, mile 38.6	Rw	72.0	

SHENANDOAH NATIONAL PARK

G B S	North to South	FEATURES	Facilities (See page xv for codes)	South to North	G B S
	Miles from Front Royal, Va.		*Miles from Rockfish Gap, Va.*		
	36.5	Side trail to Stony Man summit		70.4	
◆	36.9	Skyland Service Road (north) (L,M 0.3m W)	RLM	70.0	◆
	37.7	Skyland Service Road (south)	R	69.2	
	39.7	Side trail to Crescent Rock Overlook; Skyline Drive, mile 44.4		67.2	
SNP 4	40.2	Hawksbill Gap; Skyline Drive, mile 45.6	R	66.7	SNP 4
	41.2	Side trail to Hawksbill Mountain, Byrd's Nest #2 Picnic Shelter (0.9m E)		65.7	
	41.5	Rock Spring Cabin (locked) & Hut (S,w 0.2m W)	Sw	65.4	
◆	43.4	Fishers Gap; Skyline Drive, mile 49.3	R	63.5	◆
	44.4	David Spring	w	62.5	
	44.9	Big Meadows (C,L,M 0.1m E)	RCLM	62.0	
	45.9	Big Meadows Wayside, Harry F. Byrd, Sr., Visitor Center (w on A.T.; G,M 0.4m E)	RGMw	61.0	
	46.7	Spring	w	60.2	
	47.6	Milam Gap; Skyline Drive, mile 52.8	R	59.3	
SNP 5	49.5	Hazeltop		57.4	SNP 5
	50.4	Bootens Gap; Skyline Drive, mile 55.1	R	56.5	
	52.9	Bearfence Mountain Hut (S,w 0.1m E)	Sw	54.0	
	53.8	Lewis Mountain Campground; Skyline Drive, mile 57.6 (C,G,L,w 0.1m W)	RCGLw	53.1	
	55.4	Spring	w	51.5	
	55.7	Pocosin Cabin (locked)	w	51.2	
	59.0	South River Picnic Grounds (w 0.1m W)	w	47.9	

SHENANDOAH NATIONAL PARK

G B S	North to South	FEATURES	Facilities (See page xv for codes)	South to North	G B S
	Miles from Front Royal, Va.			*Miles from Rockfish Gap, Va.*	
◆	62.0	Swift Run Gap, U.S. 33;			◆
		Skyline Drive, mile 65.5	R	44.9	
	63.3	Skyline Drive, mile 66.7	R	43.6	
	64.7	Hightop Mountain		42.2	
	64.9	Spring	w	42.0	
SNP 6	65.4	Hightop Hut			SNP 6
		(S 0.1m W; w 0.2m W)	Sw	41.5	
	66.7	Smith Roach Gap;			
		Skyline Drive, mile 68.6	R	40.2	
	67.8	Little Roundtop Mountain		39.1	
	68.3	Powell Gap; Skyline Drive, mile 69.9	R	38.6	
◆	71.6	Simmons Gap; Skyline Drive, mile 73.2	Rw	35.3	◆
	73.5	Pinefield Gap; Skyline Drive, mile 75.2	R	33.4	
	73.7	Pinefield Hut	Sw	33.2	
	75.3	Ivy Creek Overlook;			
		Skyline Drive, mile 77.5	R	31.6	
	77.4	Spring	w	29.5	
SNP 7	79.5	Loft Mountain Campground			SNP 7
		(C,G,M, w 0.2m W)	CGMw	27.4	
	81.6	Doyles River Cabin (locked);			
		Skyline Drive, mile 81.1			
		(w 0.3m E)	Rw	25.3	
	82.5	Doyles River Parking Overlook;			
		Skyline Drive, mile 81.9	R	24.4	
	82.9	Skyline Drive, mile 82.2	R	24.0	
◆	83.8	Browns Gap; Skyline Drive, mile 82.9	R	23.1	◆
	85.2	Skyline Drive, mile 84.3	R	21.7	
	86.2	Blackrock		20.7	
SNP 8	86.8	Blackrock Hut			SNP 8
		(S,w 0.2m E)	Sw	20.1	
	87.3	Skyline Drive, mile 87.2	R	19.6	
	87.5	Blackrock Gap; Skyline Drive, mile 87.4	R	19.4	
	89.3	Skyline Drive, mile 88.9	R	17.6	

SHENANDOAH NATIONAL PARK

G B S	North to South	FEATURES	Facilities (See page xv for codes)	South to North	G B S
	Miles from Front Royal, Va.			*Miles from Rockfish Gap, Va.*	
SNP 8	93.4	Skyline Drive, mile 92.4	R	13.5	SNP 8
	95.4	Turk Gap; Skyline Drive, mile 94.1	R	11.5	
	97.0	Skyline Drive, mile 95.3	R	9.9	
	98.7	Spring	w	8.2	
◆	98.9	Jarman Gap; Skyline Drive, mile 96.9; southern boundary, Shenandoah National Park	R	8.0	◆
	99.3	Spring	w	7.6	
	99.9	Calf Mountain Shelter (w 0.2m W; S 0.3m W)	Sw	7.0	
SNP 9	101.4	Beagle Gap; Skyline Drive, mile 99.5	R	5.5	SNP 9
	102.0	Bear Den Mountain		4.9	
	103.2	McCormick Gap; Skyline Drive, mile 102.1	R	3.7	
	106.1	Self-registration station for SNP camping permits, park entrance station (0.2m W)		0.8	
	106.7	Skyline Drive, mile 105.2	R	0.2	
	106.8	I-64 Overpass	R	0.1	
	106.9	Rockfish Gap, U.S. 250, I-64; **Waynesboro, Va., P.O. 22980** (P.O.,G,L,M 4.5m W; G,L,M on A.T.)	RGLM	0.0	

Central Virginia

G B S	North to South	FEATURES	Facilities (See page xv for codes)	South to North	G B S
	Miles from **Rockfish Gap, Va.**			**Miles from** **New River, Va.**	
◆	0.0	Rockfish Gap, U.S. 250, I-64; **Waynesboro, Va., P.O. 22980** (P.O.,G,L,M 4.5m W; G,L,M on A.T.)	RGLM	220.6	◆
	4.9	Mill Creek, Paul C. Wolfe Shelter	Sw	215.7	
	6.8	Humpback Rocks Parking Area; Blue Ridge Parkway, mile 6.0 (w 0.3m W)	Rw	213.8	
Va. 15	7.6	Humpback Rocks		213.0	Va. 15
	8.6	Humpback Mountain		212.0	
	11.6	Dripping Rock Parking Area; Blue Ridge Parkway, mile 9.6	Rw	209.0	
	12.1	Cedar Cliff		208.5	
	15.9	Three Ridges Parking Overlook; Blue Ridge Parkway, mile 13.1	R	204.7	
◆	16.4	Reeds Gap, Va. 664; Blue Ridge Parkway, mile 13.6	R	204.2	◆
Va. 16	18.1	Maupin Field Shelter	Sw	202.5	Va. 16
	20.1	Hanging Rock Overlook		200.5	
	22.3	Chimney Rocks		198.3	
	24.3	Harpers Creek Shelter	Sw	196.3	
◆	26.9	Tye River, Va. 56; **Tyro, Va., P.O. 22976** (P.O.,G 1.4m E; C on A.T.; G 1.1m W)	RCG	193.7	◆
	28.2	Cripple Creek	w	192.4	
	31.2	The Priest		189.4	
	31.7	The Priest Shelter	Sw	188.9	
Va. 17	32.6	Crabtree Farm Road (Va. 826), Crabtree Falls Trail (C,w 0.5m W)	RCw	188.0	Va. 17
	33.4	Cash Hollow Road	R	187.2	
	34.7	Cash Hollow Rock		185.9	
	35.5	Main Top Mountain		185.1	
	35.8	Spy Rock		184.8	

CENTRAL VIRGINIA

G B S	North to South	FEATURES	Facilities (See page xv for codes)	South to North	G B S
	Miles from Rockfish Gap, Va.			*Miles from New River, Va.*	
◆	36.3	Fish Hatchery Road; **Montebello, Va., P.O. 24464** (P.O.,C,G,L 1.9m W)	RCGL	184.3	◆
	37.5	Porters Field		183.1	
	38.4	Twin Springs	w	182.2	
Va. 18	38.7	Seeley-Woodworth Shelter	Sw	181.9	Va. 18
	39.4	Elk Pond Branch	Cw	181.2	
	40.6	North Fork of Piney River	Cw	180.0	
	42.5	Greasy Spring Road		178.1	
	43.0	USFS 246		177.6	
◆	44.2	Salt Log Gap (north), USFS 63	R	176.4	◆
	45.5	Tar Jacket Ridge		175.1	
	46.4	Hog Camp Gap, USFS 48	RCw	174.2	
Va. 19	47.7	Cold Mountain		172.9	Va. 19
	48.5	Cow Camp Gap Shelter (S,w 0.6m E)	Sw	172.1	
	49.5	Bald Knob		171.1	
◆	52.3	U.S. 60; **Buena Vista, Va., P.O. 24416** (P.O.,G,L,M 9.3m W; G 1m W)	RGLM	168.3	◆
	54.1	Brown Mountain Creek Shelter	Sw	166.5	
Va. 20	56.1	Pedlar Lake Road (USFS 38)	R	164.5	Va. 20
	58.2	Pedlar Dam		162.4	
	58.5	USFS 39, Little Irish Creek	RCw	162.1	
	60.3	Rice Mountain		160.3	
	62.2	Robinson Gap Road (Va. 607)	R	158.4	
◆	62.5	Blue Ridge Parkway, mile 51.7; Punchbowl Mountain Crossing	Rw	158.1	◆
	62.9	Punchbowl Shelter (S,w 0.2m W)	Sw	157.7	
Va. 21	63.4	Punchbowl Mountain		157.2	Va. 21
	64.5	Bluff Mountain		156.1	
	66.0	Salt Log Gap (south) (w 0.5m W)	w	154.6	

G B S	North to South	FEATURES	Facilities (See page xv for codes)	South to North	G B S
	Miles from Rockfish Gap, Va.			*Miles from New River, Va.*	
	67.1	Saddle Gap		153.5	
	68.6	Big Rocky Row		152.0	
	69.6	Fullers Rocks, Little Rocky Row		151.0	
	69.7	Rocky Row Trail		150.9	
Va. 21	71.7	Johns Hollow Shelter	Sw	148.9	Va. 21
	72.3	Va. 812 (USFS 36)	R	148.3	
	72.4	Rocky Row Run	Cw	148.2	
	73.5	Cashaw Creek	w	147.1	
	73.6	U.S. 501, Va. 130; **Glasgow, Va., P.O. 24555** (P.O.,G,M 6.4m W; C,M 3.8m E)	RCGM	147.0	
♦	74.0	U.S. 501, James River; **Big Island, Va., P.O. 24526** (P.O.,G 4.6m E; G,M 4m E)	RGM	146.6	♦
Va. 22	76.6	Matts Creek Shelter	Sw	144.0	Va. 22
	78.5	Big Cove Branch	w	142.1	
	79.8	Hickory Stand, Belfast Trail		140.8	
	82.1	Marble Spring	Cw	138.5	
	83.1	High Cock Knob		137.5	
♦	84.3	Petites Gap, USFS 35; Blue Ridge Parkway, mile 71.0	R	136.3	♦
	85.7	Harrison Ground Spring	w	134.9	
	87.6	Thunder Ridge Overlook; Blue Ridge Parkway, mile 74.7	R	133.0	
Va. 23	88.0	Lower Blue Ridge Parkway crossing, mile 74.9	R	132.6	Va. 23
	89.0	Thunder Hill Shelter	Sw	131.6	
	89.3	Upper Blue Ridge Parkway crossing, mile 76.3	R	131.3	
	89.9	The Guillotine		130.7	
	90.2	Apple Orchard Mountain		130.4	
♦	91.6	Parkers Gap Road (USFS 812); Blue Ridge Parkway, mile 78.4	R	129.0	♦
Va. 24	93.4	Black Rock		127.2	Va. 24

CENTRAL VIRGINIA

GBS	North to South	FEATURES	Facilities (See page xv for codes)	South to North	GBS
	Miles from Rockfish Gap, Va.			*Miles from New River, Va.*	
	94.3	Cornelius Creek Shelter	Sw	126.3	
	94.9	Floyd Mountain		125.7	
Va. 24	99.1	Bryant Ridge Shelter (S,w 0.2m W)	Sw	121.5	Va. 24
	99.6	Va. 714 (Middle Creek-North Creek Road) (C,G 1.4m E)	RCG	121.0	
	100.9	Fork Mountain		119.7	
◆	102.5	Va. 614, Jennings Creek (w 0.3m E; L,M 4.5m W)	RLMw	118.1	◆
Va. 25	104.0	Buchanan Trail		116.6	Va. 25
	105.8	Cove Mountain Shelter	S(nw)	114.8	
	107.5	Cove Mountain		113.1	
◆	108.9	Bearwallow Gap, Va. 43, Va. 695; Blue Ridge Parkway, mile 90.9; **Buchanan, Va., P.O. 24066** (P.O.,G,M 5m W; C,G,L,M 4.9m E)	RCGLM	111.7	◆
	110.7	Blue Ridge Parkway, mile 92.5; Peaks of Otter Overlook	R	109.9	
Va. 26	111.4	Bobblets Gap Shelter (S,w 0.2mW)	Sw	109.2	Va. 26
	113.8	Blue Ridge Parkway, mile 95.3; Harveys Knob Overlook	R	106.8	
	114.4	Blue Ridge Parkway, mile 95.9; Montvale Overlook	R	106.2	
	115.5	Blue Ridge Parkway, mile 97.0; Taylors Mountain Overlook	R	105.1	
◆	116.3	Black Horse Gap, Old Fincastle Road (USFS 186); Blue Ridge Parkway, mile 97.7	R	104.3	◆
Va. 27	118.3	Spring	w	102.3	Va. 27
	118.7	Wilson Creek Shelter	Sw	101.9	
	119.4	Wilson Creek	w	101.2	

G B S	North to South	FEATURES	Facilities (See page xv for codes)	South to North	G B S
	Miles from Rockfish Gap, Va.			*Miles from New River, Va.*	
	121.3	Curry Creek	w	99.3	
	122.1	Salt Pond Road (USFS 191)	R	98.5	
	124.5	Spring	w	96.1	
Va. 27	124.9	Fullhardt Knob Shelter	Sw	95.7	Va. 27
	127.8	Va. 652	R	92.8	
	128.4	Norfolk & Western Railway, U.S. 11; **Troutville, Va., P.O. 24175** (P.O.,G 0.8m W)	RG	92.2	
◆	128.7	Va. 779, I-81	R	91.9	◆
	129.9	U.S. 220, Va. 816; **Daleville, Va., P.O. 24083; Cloverdale, Va., P.O. 24077** (P.O. 1.2m W; P.O.,G,L,M 2.3m E; G,L,M on A.T.)	RGLM	90.7	
	130.4	Tinker Creek		90.2	
	133.9	Hay Rock, Tinker Ridge		86.7	
	135.0	Angels Gap		85.6	
	139.0	Lamberts Meadow Campsite, Sawmill Run	Cw	81.6	
Va. 28	139.3	Lamberts Meadow Shelter	Sw	81.3	Va. 28
	139.9	Scorched Earth Gap, Andy Layne Trail		80.7	
	140.4	Tinker Cliffs		80.2	
	142.2	Brickey's Gap		78.4	
	145.3	Campbell Shelter	Sw	75.3	
	145.4	Pig Farm Campsite	Cw	75.2	
	146.0	McAfee Knob		74.6	
	147.5	Catawba Mountain Shelter	Sw	73.1	
	148.5	Boy Scout Shelter	S	72.1	
	149.5	Va. 311; **Catawba, Va., P.O. 24070** (P.O.,G 1m W; M 1.3m W)	RGM	71.1	
	153.8	Va. 785	R	66.8	
◆	155.4	Va. 624, North Mountain Trail (G 0.4m W)	RG	65.2	◆

CENTRAL VIRGINIA

G B S	North to South	FEATURES	Facilities (See page xv for codes)	South to North	G B S
	Miles from Rockfish Gap, Va.			*Miles from New River, Va.*	
	156.4	Rawies Rest		64.2	
	156.9	Lost Spectacles Gap		63.7	
Va. 29	157.9	Dragons Tooth, Cove Mountain		62.7	Va. 29
	161.4	Pickle Branch Shelter			
		(S,w 0.5m E)	Sw	59.2	
	162.4	Trout Creek, Va. 620	R	58.2	
	166.2	Audie Murphy Monument		54.4	
♦	170.0	Craig Creek Valley, Va. 621	R	50.6	♦
	171.3	Niday Shelter	Sw	49.3	
	172.0	Cabin Branch	Cw	48.6	
Va. 30	173.7	Sinking Creek Mountain		46.9	Va. 30
	177.3	Sarver Cabin			
		(C,w 0.3m E)	Cw	43.3	
	180.3	Va. 630, Sinking Creek	Rw	40.3	
♦	181.2	Sinking Creek Valley, Va. 42	R	39.4	♦
	182.6	Spring	w	38.0	
Va. 31	183.6	Laurel Creek Shelter	Sw	37.0	Va. 31
	186.6	Rocky Gap, Va. 601	R	34.0	
	187.6	Stream	w	33.0	
♦	188.6	Johns Creek Valley, USFS 156	Rw	32.0	♦
	189.4	War Spur Shelter	Sw	31.2	
	192.5	Campsites, spring	Cw	28.1	
	193.7	Wind Rock		26.9	
Va. 32	193.9	Salt Sulphur Turnpike (Va. 613)	R	26.7	Va. 32
	197.8	Bailey Gap Shelter	S	23.0	
	197.8	Spring	w	22.8	
	199.1	Va. 635, Stony Creek	R	21.5	
	200.1	Dismal Branch	w	20.5	
♦	201.2	Va. 635, Stony Creek Valley	R	19.4	♦
	201.5	Pine Swamp Branch Shelter	Sw	19.1	
Va. 33	204.0	Pine Swamp Ridge, Allegheny Trail		16.6	Va. 33
	206.4	Dickinson Gap		14.2	

G B S	North to South	FEATURES	Facilities (See page xv for codes)	South to North	G B S
	Miles from Rockfish Gap, Va.			*Miles from New River, Va.*	
Va. 33	207.9	Groundhog Trail		12.7	Va. 33
	208.9	Symms Gap Meadow		11.7	
	212.4	Campsite, water	Cw	8.2	
	213.8	Rice Field Shelter	Sw	6.8	
	216.6	Springs	Cw	4.0	
	218.8	Stillhouse Branch Road (Va. 641)	R	1.8	
	220.6	U.S. 460, Senator Shumate Bridge (east end), New River (G 0.1m E)	RG	0.0	

Southwest Virginia

G B S	North to South	FEATURES	Facilities (See page xv for codes)	South to North	G B S
	Miles from *New River, Va.*			*Miles from* *Damascus, Va.*	
◆	0.0	U.S. 460, Senator Shumate Bridge (east end), New River (G 0.1m E)	RG	162.6	◆
	0.5	**Pearisburg, Va., P.O. 24134** (P.O.,G,M 1m E; L 2m E)	RGLM	162.1	
	1.0	Va. 634	R	161.6	
	1.2	Spring	w	161.4	
	2.5	Angels Rest, Pearis Mountain		160.1	
Va. 34	3.0	Campsite, spring	Cw	159.6	Va. 34
	8.3	Doc's Knob Shelter	Sw	154.3	
	10.5	Sugar Run Gap, Sugar Run Road	R	152.1	
	12.1	Big Horse Gap, USFS 103	R	150.5	
	12.2	Ribble Trail, north junction	w	150.4	
	16.7	Wapiti Shelter	Sw	145.9	
	18.2	Stream	w	144.4	
	18.6	Ribble Trail, south junction		144.0	
	22.5	Dismal Creek Falls Trail		140.1	
◆ Va. 35 ◆	23.6	Va. 606 (G,M,w 0.2m W)	RGMw	139.0	◆ Va. 35 ◆
	23.9	Kimberling Creek		138.7	
	29.1	Va. 608, Lickskillet Hollow (G 0.8m E)	RG	133.5	
	30.3	Jenny Knob Shelter	Sw	132.3	
	32.0	Brushy Mountain		130.6	
Va. 36	33.4	Va. 611	R	129.2	Va. 36
	40.1	Helveys Mill Shelter (S,w 0.3m E)	Sw	122.5	
	41.5	Va. 612, Kimberling Creek	Rw	121.1	
	41.8	I-77 Crossing	R	120.8	

Note: Sections in this chapter were renumbered for 1995. To coordinate with the first edition of the Southwest Virginia guidebook, subtract 6 from the section number here (e.g., Va. 34 here is Va. 28 in the guidebook).

G B S	North to South	FEATURES	Facilities (See page xv for codes)	South to North	G B S
	Miles from New River, Va.			*Miles from Damascus, Va.*	
◆	42.4	U.S. 21/52; **Bastian, Va., P.O. 24314; Bland, Va., P.O. 24315** (P.O.,G 1.8m W; P.O.,G,L,M 2.5m E)	RGLM	120.2	◆
Va. 37	49.3	Va. 615, Laurel Creek	RC	113.3	Va. 37
	49.6	Little Wolf Creek	w	113.0	
	53.1	Brushy Mountain		109.5	
	54.4	Jenkins Shelter	Sw	108.2	
	57.1	Davis Farm Campsite (C,w 0.5m W)	Cw	105.5	
	57.2	Garden Mountain		105.4	
◆	58.0	Va. 623	R	104.6	◆
	62.9	Walker Gap	w	99.7	
	64.2	Chestnut Knob Shelter	S(nw)	98.4	
Va. 38	66.0	Spring-fed pond	w	96.6	Va. 38
	68.8	USFS 222	R	93.8	
	71.3	Lynn Camp Mountain		91.3	
	72.8	Stream	w	89.8	
	73.2	Knot Maul Branch Shelter	S	89.4	
◆	75.3	Va. 42; **Ceres, Va., P.O. 24318** (P.O. 5.2m E; w 0.2m E)	Rw	87.3	◆
	77.7	Va. 610	R	84.9	
Va. 39	79.3	Tilson Gap, Big Walker Mountain		83.3	Va. 39
	81.0	Crawfish Valley (C,w 0.3m E)	Cw	81.6	
	82.1	Gullion (Little Brushy) Mountain		80.5	
	84.6	Davis Path Shelter	S(nw)	78.0	
	86.2	Va. 617	R	76.4	
◆	87.3	Va. 683, U.S. 11, I-81; **Atkins, Va., P.O. 24311** (P.O.,G,M 3.2m W; G,L,M on A.T.)	RGLM	75.3	◆
Va. 40	89.4	Va. 729	R	73.2	Va. 40
	90.0	Va. 615	R	72.6	

Southwest Virginia

Appalachian Trail Data Book–1997

G B S	North to South	FEATURES	Facilities (See page xv for codes)	South to North	G B S
	Miles from New River, Va.		*Miles from Damascus, Va.*		
Va. 40	91.5	USFS 644	R	71.1	Va. 40
	91.8	Chatfield Shelter	Sw	70.8	
	93.8	Glade Mountain		68.8	
	94.7	USFS 86	Rw	67.9	
	95.1	Locust Mountain		67.5	
	97.6	Brushy Mountain		65.0	
	98.1	Va. 622	R	64.5	
♦	98.8	Va. 16, Brushy Mountain; **Sugar Grove, Va., P.O. 24375** (P.O.,G,M 3.2m E; G 3m W)	RGM	63.8	♦
Va. 41	102.8	Va. 601	R	59.8	Va. 41
	106.8	Va. 670, South Fork Holston River	R	55.8	
	107.9	Va. 672	R	54.7	
	109.4	Trimpi Shelter	Sw	53.2	
	111.3	High Point		51.3	
	111.9	Raccoon Branch Shelter (S,w 0.2m E)	Sw	50.7	
♦	113.4	Dickey Gap, Va. 16, Va. 650; **Troutdale, Va., P.O. 24378** (P.O. 2.6m E; L 4.1m E)	RL	49.2	♦
Va. 42	114.6	Comers Creek	w	48.0	Va. 42
	115.5	Hurricane Campground Side Trail (C 0.5m W)	C	47.1	
	117.2	Stream	w	45.4	
	118.0	Stream	w	44.6	
	119.6	Chestnut Flats, Iron Mountain Trail		43.0	
	119.9	Iron Mountain		42.7	
♦	121.9	Va. 603, Fox Creek (w on A.T.; C,w 2m W)	RCw	40.7	♦
Va. 43	123.6	Old Orchard Shelter	Sw	39.0	Va. 43
	125.3	Pine Mountain		37.3	
	127.0	Stone Mountain		35.6	
	128.3	Spring	w	34.3	

G B S	North to South	FEATURES	Facilities (See page xv for codes)	South to North	G B S
	Miles from New River, Va.			*Miles from Damascus, Va.*	
	129.4	Grayson Highlands Park, Wise Shelter (S,w on A.T.; C,w 2m E)	CSw	33.2	
Va. 43	132.5	Wilburn Ridge		30.1	Va. 43
	133.8	Rhododendron Gap		28.8	
	134.6	Thomas Knob Shelter	Sw	28.0	
	135.0	Susan Spillane Trail to Mt. Rogers		27.6	
	137.0	Deep Gap	w	25.6	
◆	138.8	Va. 600, Elk Garden; **Whitetop, Va., P.O. 24292** (P.O.,G 3.4m E; G,M 3.5m W)	RGM	23.8	◆
Va. 44	139.3	Stream	w	23.3	Va. 44
	141.2	Whitetop Mountain Road	RC	21.4	
	142.0	Buzzard Rock, Whitetop Mountain		20.6	
	144.5	Va. 601	Rw	18.1	
◆	145.7	U.S. 58; **Summit Cut, Va.**	R	16.9	◆
	146.8	Lost Mountain Shelter	Sw	15.8	
	147.8	Stream	w	14.8	
	148.0	Va. 859, Whitetop Laurel Creek	R	14.6	
	148.6	Virginia Creeper Trail		14.0	
	149.1	Va. 728, Creek Junction Station	R	13.5	
	150.9	Campsite	C	11.7	
	152.1	Stream	w	10.5	
Va. 45	153.2	Saunders Shelter (S,w 0.2m W)	Sw	9.4	Va. 45
	153.5	Straight Mountain		9.1	
	155.0	Taylors Valley Side Trail		7.6	
	155.7	Stream	w	6.9	
	157.0	U.S. 58, Straight Branch, Feathercamp Branch	Rw	5.6	
	159.1	Feathercamp Ridge, Iron Mountain Trail		3.5	
	161.6	U.S. 58, Virginia Creeper Trail	R	1.0	
	162.6	**Damascus, Va., P.O. 24236** (P.O.,G,L,M on A.T.)	RGLM	0.0	

Tennessee-North Carolina

GBS	North to South	FEATURES	Facilities (See page xv for codes)	South to North	GBS
	Miles from Damascus, Va.			*Miles from Fontana Dam, N.C.*	
◆	0.0	**Damascus, Va., P.O. 24236**			◆
		(P.O.,G,L,M on A.T.)	RGLM	288.8	
Tenn.-N.C. 1	1.9	Spring	w	286.9	Tenn.-N.C. 1
	3.5	Virginia-Tennessee Line		285.3	
	10.0	Abingdon Gap Shelter	Sw	278.8	
	11.1	McQueens Gap, USFS 69	R	277.7	
	11.5	McQueens Knob		277.3	
	12.5	Spring	w	276.3	
◆	14.8	Low Gap, U.S. 421; **Shady Valley, Tenn., P.O. 37688**			◆
Tenn.-N.C. 2		(w on A.T.; P.O.,G,L,M 3m E)	RGLMw	274.0	Tenn.-N.C. 2
	14.9	Campsite	C	273.9	
	18.3	Double Springs Shelter, Holston Mountain Trail	Sw	270.5	
	19.3	Campsite	Cw	269.5	
◆	21.8	Tenn. 91	R	267.0	◆
	25.0	Nick Grindstaff Monument		263.8	
Tenn.-N.C. 3	26.3	Iron Mountain Shelter	S(nw)	262.5	Tenn.-N.C. 3
	26.5	Spring	w	262.3	
	28.0	Turkeypen Gap		260.8	
	29.2	Campsite	Cw	259.6	
	33.3	Vandeventer Shelter (S on A.T.; w 0.5m W)	Sw	255.5	
	35.1	Spring	w	253.7	
◆	37.8	Watauga Dam Road	R	251.0	◆
	39.0	Watauga Dam		249.8	
Tenn.-N.C. 4	40.0	Watauga Lake Shelter	Sw	248.8	Tenn.-N.C. 4
	40.3	Griffith Branch	Cw	248.5	
	41.7	U.S. 321; **Hampton, Tenn., P.O. 37658** (P.O.,G,M 2.6m W;			
		G,L 1.8m W)	RCGLM	247.1	
	44.9	Pond Flats	Cw	243.9	
	47.9	Side trail to U.S. 321	w	240.9	

TENNESSEE-NORTH CAROLINA

G B S	North to South	FEATURES	Facilities (See page xv for codes)	South to North	G B S
	Miles from Damascus, Va.		*Miles from Fontana Dam, N.C.*		
	48.7	Laurel Fork Shelter	Sw	240.1	
	49.4	Laurel Falls	w	239.4	
♦	50.6	Dennis Cove, USFS 50 (C,w 1m E)	RCw	238.2	♦
	52.3	Trail to Coon Den Falls		236.5	
	53.4	White Rocks Mountain Fire Tower		235.4	
	54.2	Campsite	Cw	234.6	
Tenn.-N.C. 5	56.4	Moreland Gap Shelter	Sw	232.4	Tenn.-N.C. 5
	57.8	Campsite	Cw	231.0	
	61.0	Campsite	Cw	227.8	
	61.5	Laurel Fork		227.3	
	62.2	Campsite	Cw	226.6	
	63.3	Walnut Mountain Road	R	225.5	
	66.5	Campbell Hollow Road	R	222.3	
	67.2	Buck Mountain Road	R	221.6	
	68.1	Spring	w	220.7	
	69.7	Bear Branch Road	R	219.1	
♦	70.0	U.S. 19E; **Roan Mountain, Tenn., P.O. 37687; Elk Park, N.C., P.O. 28622** (P.O.,G,L,M 3.4m W; P.O. 2.5m E; C 3.5m E; G 1.2m E; L 3m E; M 0.8m E, 2m E)	RCGLM	218.8	♦
	70.5	Apple House Shelter	S	218.3	
Tenn.-N.C. 6	70.6	Spring	w	218.2	Tenn.-N.C. 6
	73.0	Doll Flats	Cw	215.8	
	75.4	Hump Mountain		213.4	
	76.3	Bradley Gap	Cw	212.5	
	76.9	Little Hump Mountain	C	211.9	
	78.7	Yellow Mountain Gap, Overmountain Shelter (C on A.T.; w 0.2m E; S 0.3m E)	CSw	210.1	
	80.4	Stan Murray Shelter	Sw	208.4	
	81.8	Side trail to Grassy Ridge	Cw	207.0	
♦	83.4	Carvers Gap, Tenn. 143, N.C. 261	Rw	205.4	♦

Tennessee-North Carolina

G B S	North to South	FEATURES	Facilities (See page xv for codes)	South to North	G B S

	Miles from Damascus, Va.		*Miles from Fontana Dam, N.C.*		
Tenn.- N.C. 7	84.7	Roan High Knob Shelter	Sw	204.1	**Tenn.- N.C. 7**
	85.3	Side trail to Roan High Bluff	Rw	203.5	
◆	86.2	Ash Gap	Cw	202.6	◆
Tenn.-N.C. 8	88.0	Hughes Gap			**Tenn.-N.C. 8**
		(G 3.2m W; C,L 2m E)	RCGL	200.8	
	89.3	Little Rock Knob		199.5	
	90.1	Clyde Smith Shelter	Sw	198.7	
	91.2	Campsite	Cw	197.6	
	92.0	Greasy Creek Gap			
		(C,w 0.2m W)	Cw	196.8	
◆	94.6	Stream	w	194.2	◆
	96.1	Iron Mountain Gap, Tenn. 107, N.C. 226			
		(G 0.5m E)	RG	192.7	
	97.3	Little Bald Knob		191.5	
	98.8	Cherry Gap Shelter	Sw	190.0	
	99.8	Low Gap	w	189.0	
Tenn.-N.C. 9	101.5	Unaka Mountain		187.3	**Tenn.-N.C. 9**
	102.5	USFS 230	R	186.3	
	103.1	Deep Gap	Cw	185.7	
	104.4	Beauty Spot Gap	RCw	184.4	
	104.6	Beauty Spot		184.2	
	105.8	USFS 230	R	183.0	
	106.9	Indian Grave Gap			
		(C 3.3m W)	RC	181.9	
	111.0	Curley Maple Gap Shelter	Sw	177.8	
	113.9	Nolichucky Expeditions			
		(C,L,M,S on A.T.)	RCLMS	174.9	
◆	115.2	Nolichucky River;			◆
		Erwin, Tenn., P.O. 37650			
Tenn.- N.C. 10		(P.O.,L,M 3.8m W; G 2.3m W)	RGLM	173.6	**Tenn.- N.C. 10**
	119.1	Temple Hill Gap		169.7	
	121.5	No Business Knob Shelter	S	167.3	
	121.7	Spring	w	167.1	

TENNESSEE-NORTH CAROLINA

G B S	North to South	FEATURES	Facilities (See page xv for codes)	South to North	G B S
	Miles from Damascus, Va.		*Miles from Fontana Dam, N.C.*		
	125.4	Ogelsby Branch	w	163.4	
◆	126.2	Spivey Gap, U.S. 19W (C,w 0.5m W)	RCw	162.6	◆
	126.7	Campsite	Cw	162.1	
	127.8	Trail to High Rocks		161.0	
	128.5	Whistling Gap	Cw	160.3	
Tenn.-N.C. 11	130.5	Little Bald		158.3	Tenn.-N.C. 11
	131.5	Campsite	Cw	157.3	
	131.9	Bald Mountain Shelter	Sw	156.9	
	132.8	Big Stamp (C,w 0.3m W; M 1.5m E)	CMw	156.0	
	133.0	Big Bald		155.8	
	133.8	Spring	w	155.0	
	135.8	Low Gap	Cw	153.0	
	137.2	Street Gap		151.6	
	138.8	Springs	w	150.0	
◆	139.8	Sams Gap, U.S. 23 (G 3.2m E; M 2.8m E)	RGM	149.0	◆
Tenn.-N.C. 12	141.5	High Rock		147.3	Tenn.-N.C. 12
	142.0	Hogback Ridge Shelter (S 0.1m E; w 0.3m E)	Sw	146.8	
	143.1	Rice Gap	R	145.7	
	144.1	Big Flat	Cw	144.7	
	144.7	Frozen Knob		144.1	
	147.5	Boone Cove Road	R	141.3	
◆	148.0	Devil Fork Gap, N.C. 212	R	140.8	◆
	149.8	Campsite	Cw	139.0	
Tenn.-N.C. 13	150.7	Flint Mountain Shelter	Sw	138.1	Tenn.-N.C. 13
	153.4	Spring	w	135.4	
	154.7	Big Butt	C	134.1	
	156.6	Jerry Cabin Shelter	Sw	132.2	
	159.1	Spring	w	129.7	
	160.0	Blackstack Cliffs		128.8	

Tennessee-North Carolina

G B S	North to South	FEATURES	Facilities (See page xv for codes)	South to North	G B S
	Miles from Damascus, Va.		*Miles from Fontana Dam, N.C.*		
Tenn.-N.C. 13	160.3	Spring	w	128.5	Tenn.-N.C. 13
	162.0	Camp Creek Bald, side trail to fire tower	R	126.8	
	163.3	Little Laurel Shelter	Sw	125.5	
	166.6	Old Hayesville Road	R	122.2	
◆	168.2	Allen Gap, N.C. 208, Tenn. 70 (w on A.T.)	Rw	120.6	◆
Tenn.-N.C. 14	170.4	Spring	w	118.4	Tenn.-N.C. 14
	171.9	Spring Mountain Shelter	Sw	116.9	
	173.6	Hurricane Gap	R	115.2	
	174.6	Rich Mountain Fire Tower Side Trail	Cw	114.2	
	177.0	Tanyard Gap, U.S. 25 & 70	R	111.8	
	178.0	Campsite	Cw	110.8	
	179.6	Pump Gap		109.2	
	181.5	Lovers Leap Rock		107.3	
◆	182.9	U.S. 25 & 70, N.C. 209; **Hot Springs, N.C., P.O. 28743** (P.O.,G,L,M on A.T.)	RGLM	105.9	◆
Tenn.-N.C. 15	186.1	Deer Park Mountain Shelter	Sw	102.7	Tenn.-N.C. 15
	189.5	Garenflo Gap	R	99.3	
	191.8	Big Rock Spring	w	97.0	
	193.2	Bluff Mountain		95.6	
	195.6	Spring	w	93.2	
	196.9	Lemon Gap, N.C. 1182, Tenn. 107	R	91.9	
	197.4	Roaring Fork Shelter	Sw	91.4	
	202.3	Max Patch Summit		86.5	
◆	203.1	Max Patch Road (N.C. 1182)	R	85.7	◆
	205.8	Brown Gap	RCw	83.0	
Tenn.-N.C. 16	208.7	Deep Gap, Groundhog Creek Shelter (S,w 0.2m E)	Sw	80.1	Tenn.-N.C. 16
	210.7	Campsite	Cw	78.1	
	211.2	Snowbird Mountain	R	77.6	
	212.7	Spanish Oak Gap		76.1	

TENNESSEE-NORTH CAROLINA

G B S	North to South	FEATURES	Facilities (See page xv for codes)	South to North	G B S
	Miles from Damascus, Va.			*Miles from Fontana Dam, N.C.*	
Tenn.-N.C. 16	213.6	Painter Branch	Cw	75.2	Tenn.-N.C. 16
	215.9	Waterville School Road	R	72.9	
	216.5	I-40	R	72.3	
	216.7	Pigeon River		72.1	
	217.0	State Line Branch	Cw	71.8	
◆	218.3	Davenport Gap, Tenn. 32, N.C. 284; eastern boundary, Great Smoky Mountains National Park (G,L,M 1.3m E; C 2.5m E)	RCGLM	70.5	◆
Tenn.-N.C. 17	219.2	Davenport Gap Shelter	Sw	69.6	Tenn.-N.C. 17
	221.4	Spring	w	67.4	
	223.0	Spring	w	65.8	
	223.5	Mt. Cammerer Side Trail		65.3	
	226.3	Cosby Knob Shelter	Sw	62.5	
	226.8	Cosby Knob		62.0	
	230.2	Snake Den Ridge Trail		58.6	
	232.1	Mt. Guyot Side Trail		56.7	
	232.2	Guyot Spring	w	56.6	
	234.0	Tri-Corner Knob Shelter	Sw	54.8	
	235.0	Mt. Chapman		53.8	
	236.5	Mt. Sequoyah		52.3	
	239.2	Pecks Corner Shelter (w on A.T.; S,w 0.5m E)	Sw	49.6	
	240.5	Bradleys View		48.3	
	243.8	The Sawteeth		45.0	
	245.7	Charlies Bunion		43.1	
	246.6	Icewater Spring Shelter	Sw	42.2	
	246.9	Boulevard Trail		41.9	
◆	249.6	Newfound Gap, U.S. 441	Rw	39.2	◆
Tenn.-N.C. 18	251.3	Indian Gap	R	37.5	Tenn.-N.C. 18
	254.1	Mt. Collins Shelter (S,w 0.5m W)	Sw	34.7	
	256.3	Mt. Love		32.5	

Tennessee-North Carolina

G B S	North to South	FEATURES	Facilities (See page xv for codes)	South to North	G B S
	Miles from Damascus, Va.			*Miles from Fontana Dam, N.C.*	
	257.5	Clingmans Dome (R,w 0.5m E)	Rw	31.3	
	260.4	Double Spring Gap Shelter	Sw	28.4	
	261.9	Silers Bald		26.9	
	262.1	Silers Bald Shelter	Sw	26.7	
	264.8	Buckeye Gap	w	24.0	
	267.4	Sams Gap	w	21.4	
	267.6	Derrick Knob Shelter	Sw	21.2	
	268.7	Sugar Tree Gap		20.1	
	271.1	Mineral Gap		17.7	
Tenn.-N.C. 18	271.8	Beechnut Gap	w	17.0	Tenn.-N.C. 18
	272.1	Thunderhead, east peak		16.7	
	272.7	Rocky Top		16.1	
	273.9	Eagle Creek Trail to Spence Field Shelter; Bote Mountain Trail	Sw	14.9	
	276.4	Russell Field Shelter	Sw	12.4	
	277.3	Little Abrams Gap		11.5	
	278.7	Devils Tater Patch		10.1	
	279.0	Mollies Ridge Shelter	Sw	9.8	
	279.9	Ekaneetlee Gap	w	8.9	
	281.3	Doe Knob		7.5	
	283.6	Birch Spring Shelter	Sw	5.2	
	284.8	Shuckstack		4.0	
	288.8	Little Tennessee River, Fontana Dam; southern boundary, Great Smoky Mountains National Park	R	0.0	

North Carolina-Georgia

G B S	North to South	FEATURES	Facilities (See page xv for codes)	South to North	G B S
	Miles from Fontana Dam, N.C.			*Miles from Springer Mountain, Ga.*	
◆	0.0	Little Tennessee River, Fontana Dam; southern boundary, Great Smoky Mountains National Park	R	163.5	◆
	0.4	Fontana Dam Visitors Center (M,w on A.T.)	Mw	163.1	
N.C. 3	0.7	Fontana Dam Shelter	Sw	162.8	N.C. 3
	1.8	N.C. 28; **Fontana Dam, N.C., P.O. 28733** (P.O.,G,L,M 2m W)	RGLM	161.7	
	4.5	Walker Gap		159.0	
	5.9	Black Gum Gap		157.6	
	7.3	Cable Gap Shelter	Sw	156.2	
◆	8.2	Yellow Creek Gap, Yellow Creek Mountain Road (L 4m E)	RL	155.3	◆
N.C. 4	10.6	Cody Gap	w	152.9	N.C. 4
	11.4	Hogback Gap		152.1	
	13.2	Brown Fork Gap	w	150.3	
	13.4	Brown Fork Gap Shelter	Sw	150.1	
	14.8	Sweetwater Gap		148.7	
◆	15.8	Stecoah Gap, Sweetwater Creek Road (N.C. 143)	Rw	147.7	◆
	17.9	Simp Gap		145.6	
N.C. 5	18.9	Locust Cove Gap	w	144.6	N.C. 5
	21.3	Cheoah Bald		142.2	
	22.5	Sassafras Gap Shelter	Sw	141.0	
	23.4	Swim Bald	Cw	140.1	
	26.3	Grassy Gap	w	137.2	
	27.8	Wright Gap		135.7	
◆	29.4	U.S. 19, Nantahala River; **Wesser, N.C.** (G,L,M on A.T.)	RGLM	134.1	◆
N.C. 6	30.2	A. Rufus Morgan Shelter	Sw	133.3	N.C. 6
	33.5	Jumpup Lookout		130.0	
	35.1	Wesser Creek Trail, Wesser Bald Shelter	S	128.4	

NORTH CAROLINA-GEORGIA

G B S	North to South	FEATURES	Facilities (See page xv for codes)	South to North	G B S
	Miles from Fontana Dam, N.C.		*Miles from Springer Mountain, Ga.*		
	35.2	Spring	w	128.3	
	35.9	Wesser Bald		127.6	
♦	37.3	Tellico Gap, N.C. 1365	R	126.2	♦
	38.7	Campsite	Cw	124.8	
	39.0	Side trail to Rocky Bald Lookout		124.5	
	40.2	Copper Ridge Bald Lookout		123.3	
	40.9	Cold Spring Shelter	Sw	122.6	
N.C. 7	42.1	Burningtown Gap, N.C. 1397	R	121.4	N.C. 7
	44.4	Licklog Gap			
		(C on A.T.; w 0.5m W)	Cw	119.1	
	46.2	Campsite	Cw	117.3	
	46.6	Wayah Bald	R	116.9	
	48.5	Wine Spring	Cw	115.0	
	49.0	USFS 69	Rw	114.5	
♦	50.8	Wayah Gap, N.C. 1310	R	112.7	♦
	53.0	Siler Bald Shelter			
		(S,w 0.5m E)	Sw	110.5	
N.C. 8	54.7	Panther Gap	C	108.8	N.C. 8
	55.8	Campsites	Cw	107.7	
	56.7	Winding Stair Gap, U.S. 64;			
		Franklin, N.C., P.O. 28734			
		(w on A.T.; P.O.,G,L,M 10m E)	RGLMw	106.8	
♦	59.8	Wallace Gap, Old U.S. 64			♦
		(C,G,L 1m W)	RCGL	103.7	
	60.4	Rock Gap, Standing Indian Campground			
		(C 1.5m W)	RC	103.1	
N.C. 9	60.5	Rock Gap Shelter	Sw	103.0	N.C. 9
	63.0	Glassmine Gap		100.5	
	65.8	Big Spring Shelter	Sw	97.7	
	66.4	Albert Mountain		97.1	
	66.7	Bear Pen Trail, USFS 67	R	96.8	
	67.8	Spring	w	95.7	
	68.0	Mooney Gap, USFS 83	RC	95.5	

G B S	North to South	FEATURES	Facilities (See page xv for codes)	South to North	G B S
	Miles from Fontana Dam, N.C.			*Miles from Springer Mountain, Ga.*	
	68.9	Betty Creek Gap	Cw	94.6	
	72.6	Carter Gap Shelter	CSw	90.9	
	73.0	Timber Ridge Trail		90.5	
N.C. 9	75.8	Beech Gap	Cw	87.7	N.C. 9
	78.7	Lower Trail Ridge Trail, Standing Indian Mountain (C on A.T.; w 0.2m W)	Cw	84.8	
	80.2	Standing Indian Shelter	Sw	83.3	
◆	81.1	Deep Gap, USFS 71	Rw	82.4	◆
	83.2	Wateroak Gap		80.3	
N.C. 10	84.1	Chunky Gal Trail		79.4	N.C. 10
	84.4	Whiteoak Stamp		79.1	
	85.1	Muskrat Creek Shelter	Sw	78.4	
	86.0	Sassafras Gap		77.5	
◆	87.9	Bly Gap	Cw	75.6	◆
	88.1	North Carolina-Georgia Line		75.4	
	89.9	Rich Cove Gap		73.6	
	90.1	Campsite	Cw	73.4	
	91.1	Blue Ridge Gap		72.4	
Ga. 11	91.7	As Knob		71.8	Ga. 11
	92.4	Plumorchard Gap Shelter (S 0.2m E)	Sw	71.1	
	93.5	Bull Gap		70.0	
	94.9	Cowart Gap		68.6	
	95.1	Stream	w	68.4	
	95.6	Campsite	Cw	67.9	
◆	96.7	Dicks Creek Gap, U.S. 76 (w on A.T.; L 3.5m W)	RLw	66.8	◆
Ga. 12	97.2	Streams	w	66.3	Ga. 12
	97.9	Moreland Gap		65.6	
	98.9	Powell Mountain		64.6	
	99.1	McClure Gap	C	64.4	

NORTH CAROLINA-GEORGIA

G B S	North to South	FEATURES	Facilities (See page xv for codes)	South to North	G B S
	Miles from Fontana Dam, N.C.			*Miles from Springer Mountain, Ga.*	
	100.2	Deep Gap Shelter			
		(S,w 0.3m E)	Sw	63.3	
	100.9	Kelly Knob		62.6	
	102.0	Addis Gap			
		(C,w 0.5m E)	Cw	61.5	
	102.8	Sassafras Gap	Cw	60.7	
	103.9	Blue Ridge Swag		59.6	
Ga. 12	107.3	Tray Mountain Shelter			Ga. 12
		(S 0.2m W; w 0.3m W)	Sw	56.2	
	107.6	Tray Mountain		55.9	
	108.4	Tray Gap, Tray Mountain Road (USFS 79)	R	55.1	
	109.2	Cheese Factory Site	Cw	54.3	
	109.4	Tray Mountain Road (USFS 79)	R	54.1	
	110.1	Indian Grave Gap	R	53.4	
	111.5	Rocky Mountain	C	52.0	
	112.2	Stream	w	51.3	
◆	112.8	Unicoi Gap, Ga. 75;			◆
		Helen, Ga., P.O. 30545			
		(P.O.,G,L,M 9m W)	RGLM	50.7	
	114.2	Blue Mountain		49.3	
	115.0	Blue Mountain Shelter	Sw	48.5	
	115.5	Campsite	C	48.0	
	115.7	Spring	w	47.8	
	115.9	Campsite	C	47.6	
Ga. 13	116.6	Red Clay Gap		46.9	Ga. 13
	117.2	Chattahoochee Gap	Cw	46.3	
	118.4	Cold Springs Gap		45.1	
	120.8	Poplar Stamp Gap	Cw	42.7	
	122.2	Low Gap Shelter	CSw	41.3	
	122.8	Sheep Rock Top		40.7	
	124.5	Poor Mountain		39.0	
	125.5	White Oak Stamp		38.0	
	126.4	Hogpen Gap, Ga. 348	Rw	37.1	

G B S	North to South	FEATURES	Facilities (See page xv for codes)	South to North	G B S
	Miles from *Fontana Dam, N.C.*			*Miles from* *Springer Mountain, Ga.*	
	126.6	Whitley Gap Shelter (S 1.2m E; w 1.5m E)	Sw	36.9	
♦	127.3	Tesnatee Gap, Ga. 348	R	36.2	♦
	128.1	Cowrock Mountain		35.4	
	128.6	Baggs Creek Gap	w	34.9	
	129.4	Wolf Laurel Top		34.1	
Ga. 14	129.5	Corbin Horse Stamp		34.0	Ga. 14
	130.0	Rock Spring Top	w	33.5	
	130.7	Swaim Gap		32.8	
	131.3	Levelland Mountain		32.2	
	131.7	Bull Gap	Cw	31.8	
♦	132.8	Neels Gap, U.S. 19/129 (G,L on A.T.; L 0.3m E; C,G 3m W; C,L 3.5m W)	RCGLw	30.7	♦
	133.7	Trail to Byron Reece Memorial (C 1m W; w 0.2m W)	Cw	29.8	
	135.2	Blood Mountain Shelter	S(nw)	28.3	
	136.1	Slaughter Gap	Cw	27.4	
Ga. 15	136.5	Stream	w	27.0	Ga. 15
	136.8	Bird Gap	C(nw)	26.7	
	138.2	Jarrard Gap (w 0.3m W; G 1.8m W)	Gw	25.3	
	138.7	Burnett Field Mountain		24.8	
	140.6	Campsite	Cw	22.9	
	141.3	Granny Top Mountain		22.2	
	142.5	Big Cedar Mountain		21.0	
	142.8	Lunsford Gap	C(nw)	20.7	
♦	143.5	Woody Gap, Ga. 60; **Suches, Ga., P.O. 30572** (w on A.T.; P.O.,G 2m W; G 1.6m W)	RGw	20.0	♦
Ga. 16	144.9	Ramrock Mountain		18.6	Ga. 16
	147.1	Gooch Gap, USFS 42	RCw	16.4	

NORTH CAROLINA-GEORGIA

G B S	North to South	FEATURES	Facilities (See page xv for codes)	South to North	G B S
	Miles from Fontana Dam, N.C.		*Miles from Springer Mountain, Ga.*		
	147.4	Gooch Gap Shelter (w on A.T.; S 0.2m E)	Sw	16.1	
Ga. 16	149.2	Blackwell Creek	Cw	14.3	Ga. 16
	149.9	Justus Creek	Cw	13.6	
	151.3	Justus Mountain		12.2	
	151.9	Cooper Gap, USFS 42/80	R	11.6	
	153.5	Horse Gap	R	10.0	
◆	155.4	Hightower Gap, USFS 42/69	R	8.1	◆
	155.9	Hawk Mountain Shelter (S 0.2m W; w 0.4m W)	Sw	7.6	
	157.7	Logging Road	R	5.8	
	158.5	Long Creek Falls	w	5.0	
Ga. 17	159.4	Three Forks, USFS 58	RCw	4.1	Ga. 17
	159.9	Stover Creek	w	3.6	
	161.0	Stover Creek Shelter	Sw	2.5	
	162.6	USFS 42	R	0.9	
	163.3	Springer Mountain Shelter (S,w 0.2m E)	Sw	0.2	
	163.5	Springer Mountain	C	0.0	

Amicalola Falls Approach Trail

G B S	North to South	FEATURES	Facilities (See page xv for codes)	South to North	G B S
	Miles from Springer Mountain, Ga.		*Miles from Amicalola Falls State Park*		
	0.0	Springer Mountain	C	8.1	
	1.0	Black Gap Shelter	Sw	7.1	
	2.2	Nimblewill Gap, USFS 28	R	5.9	
	3.1	Frosty Mountain Road (USFS 46)		5.0	
	3.4	Frosty Mountain	Cw	4.7	
	5.0	High Shoals Road	R	3.1	
	8.1	Visitors Center, Amicalola Falls State Park	RCLMSw	0.0	

History of the Appalachian Trail

The model for the *Appalachian Trail Data Book* was the *Mileage Fact Sheet* compiled by Ed Garvey and Gus Crews, published simultaneously in 1971 by the Appalachian Trail Conference and Appalachian Books (Oakton, Va.) as an appendix to Mr. Garvey's *Appalachian Hiker*.

The first edition (1977) of the *Appalachian Trail Data Book* was compiled by Raymond F. Hunt of Kingsport, Tenn., who continued to perform this volunteer service annually until 1983, when he began a six-year term as chair of the Appalachian Trail Conference's Board of Managers.

The 1984 and subsequent editions have been compiled by another volunteer, Daniel D. Chazin of Teaneck, N.J., an officer of the New York-New Jersey Trail Conference and editor of the *Appalachian Trail Guide to New York-New Jersey*. Mr. Chazin draws each fall on the work of ten other guidebook field editors and more than 30 other volunteer data compilers for information on the various sections of the Appalachian Trail.

INCIDENT REPORTING FORM

(Please see page xii for reporting emergencies.)

Your name _____ Today's date _____

Daytime phone # _____ Evening phone # _____

Mailing Address: _____

_____

_____

TYPE OF INCIDENT

❑ Crime (type:_____) ❑ Theft/personal property ❑ Trespass
❑ Fire   ❑ Disorderly behavior   ❑ Resource damage
❑ Search/rescue/   ❑ Drug/alcohol abuse   ❑ Dumping
  medical emergency ❑ Vandalism   ❑ ATV/ORV use
❑ Other (_____)

Date/time of incident _____

Location (please be as specific as possible: *Data Book* page, location, mileage, *etc.*) ____

_____

Who was involved? _____

_____

Witnesses_____

_____

What happened? _____

_____

_____

_____

_____

_____

_____

_____

Were law-enforcement, fire, search/rescue personnel involved/contacted? Y N

If so, which agency? _____

Name of contact there: _____

Telephone number: _____

**Please tear out this page, fold the completed form in half, and mail it to
ATC at the address on the other side (no postage necessary).**

NO POSTAGE
NECESSARY
IF MAILED
IN THE
UNITED STATES

BUSINESS REPLY MAIL
FIRST CLASS   PERMIT NO. 6   HARPERS FERRY, W.VA.

POSTAGE WILL BE PAID BY ADDRESSEE

APPALACHIAN TRAIL CONFERENCE
P.O. Box 807
Washington & Jackson Streets
Harpers Ferry, W.Va. 25425-9988